Contents

Manufactured in the United States of America
1 2 3 4 5 6 7 8 9 10

This edition published by:
Beekman House
A Division of Crown Publishers, Inc.
One Park Avenue
New York, N.Y. 10016

Library of Congress Catalog Card Number: 79-67186

Understanding the Equipment

Perhaps you own a highly sophisticated, very expensive camera; perhaps you own a simple little one that you received as a gift many years ago; and maybe you don't own a camera of any kind. That's good: This book is designed to enable all kinds of people, using all kinds of equipment, to take pleasing pictures of other people. It's certainly not limited to those of you who've spent hundreds of dollars on photographic products. As you will see, the type of camera you use is not nearly as important as the way you use it.

In this chapter we'll discuss the pros and cons of various types of equipment so that you'll be able to work effectively within the limitations of whatever you will be using. If you don't have a camera and accessories, this chapter can help you decide which kind to buy. (Refer to our chapter on product ratings for detailed information about particular brands.)

Cameras differ in many ways we won't go into here. However, for the purposes of model photography, it's important that you consider the following factors.

All other things being equal, the bigger the film used in a camera, the better the quality of the image. This film size, or format, differs greatly from one type of camera to another. A 110 camera produces a film image about half the size of a postage stamp. A 35mm camera turns out a negative or slide about four times as big as that of a 110. The film used in a 126-format camera is a bit smaller than 35mm. Medium-format, or roll-film, cameras use film that is much larger than 35. And some large-format cameras use film that is as big as this page. (Instant-film cameras are covered later in this chapter.)

Why not use the largest format you can? The answer is that the bigger the film, the bigger the camera and the higher its price. The 35mm format is regarded by many professional and advanced amateur photographers as the best compromise: easy handling, excellent image quality, and reasonable cost.

Cameras differ also in lens configuration. Only one 110 model is currently marketed with removable lenses which allow their users to increase and decrease magnification of the subject. Only one of the 35mm cameras that use the viewfinder or rangefinder viewing systems has interchangeable lenses. All single-lens-reflex, or SLR, cameras (which allow you to view the scene through the lens that takes the picture) of the 35mm and medium formats do have interchangeable-lens capability. The opportunity to change magnification becomes important to photographers who take full-figure model pictures as well as portraits; yet you can take many types of model shots with cameras having fixed lenses.

And lastly, cameras differ in their ability to be used with a wide variety of accessories such as lighting systems, automatic winding devices, and self-timers. These accessories come in handy, but they're not required for many types of model photography.

The more complex the task you set for yourself when photographing models, the more sophisticated the equipment you will need. Whichever kind of camera you own or want to own, you'll be able to take part in the enjoyable hobby of model photography.

Most modern cameras, including those with fixed lenses, have optics capable of providing high-quality enlargements to 11 x 14 inches. The 110 format remains an exception, not because the lenses are poor—equipment such as the Pentax System 10 with interchangeable lenses is excellent—but because most processing labs are still not getting optimal quality from the tiny negative. It is difficult to get consistently high-quality 8 x 10 enlargements from this format.

The 126 film format is 35mm square, and 35mm film is the size used by professionals who own Nikon, Canon, Leica, and other fine SLRs. Both formats

1

2

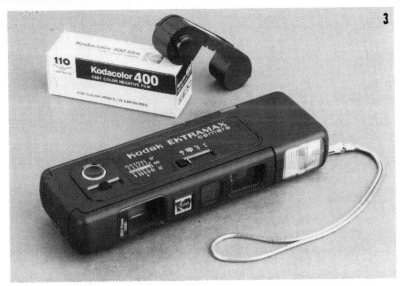

3

Full-figure photographs of people, which show the person's entire body and perhaps some of the surrounding scenery (1), can easily be handled with a 110-format camera (2). For portrait work (3), however, most photographers choose a larger format such as 35mm to maximize the clarity of the image. Generally speaking, the bigger the film size, the better the image quality.

can be handled in the same darkroom equipment; technicians who work with one can easily work with the other. Thus, good lab processing is readily available.

The price of a cheap point-and-shoot camera with a permanently attached lens is often only a fraction of the cost of a relatively inexpensive interchangeable lens for a sophisticated 35mm SLR. However, the lens of even the cheapest 110 or 126 camera available today might be equal in optical quality to some of the finest lenses of 40 years ago. And the characteristics of an optically deficient lens can work to your advantage. For example, the lack of sharpness at the edges of an enlargement made with a camera having such a lens can soften distracting details in the image.

But another kind of image can suffer if you use an inexpensive camera: your own image as a photographer. Models sometimes lack respect for photographers who use such simple equipment. They falsely equate sophisticated equipment with professionalism. (This kind of thinking causes problems for wedding photographers. Some people can have confidence in a photographer only if he is carrying a camera that appears more expensive than the one used by Uncle Ralph.)

Most photographers who want to work with models having some training wait until they own either a 35mm or a medium-format SLR. These cameras have interchangeable lenses, through-the-lens viewing for accurate framing, and built-in light meters in most cases; plus, many of them have such options

as motor drives, interchangeable viewfinders (for waist-level viewing, eye-level viewing, sports work, and other special needs), and interchangeable focusing screens.

Despite all of these capabilities, you might find that such a camera would not serve you better for many types of model photography than a less expensive one. Why pay for versatility you will never use? Model photography does not require a 250-exposure back, a microscope adapter or most of the other items offered by photographic systems manufacturers.

Many skilled photographers shun these kinds of cameras and choose instead a 35mm rangefinder or viewfinder.

The Leica rangefinder series is the most sophisticated rangefinder/viewfinder line available. Interchangeable

1

2

3

4

lenses are available, as well as a special adapter for use with a reflex housing which turns the camera into an SLR. The Leica is extremely expensive.

At this writing, all other 35mm rangefinder/viewfinder cameras have a fixed lens, but most of these lenses are focusable and are far superior to those of very inexpensive 110 and 126 cameras. Zone focusing (you guess the distance from your subject, set the lens accordingly, and hope for the best) is a nuisance. The rangefinder focusing system (the clarity of the image seen through the viewing window changes as you adjust the focus setting of the lens) is preferable, since it enables you to see whether the subject is in focus.

Medium-format equipment uses 120 roll film, taking either 4.5 × 6cm images, 6 × 6cm images (2¼ × 2¼ inches) or 2¼ × 2¾-inch images, depending upon the model. Using identical film, an 8 × 10-inch enlargement made from a medium-format negative will be superior to a print of similar size made under identical lighting and processing conditions by a 35mm camera.

Polaroid and Kodak make instant-picture films and cameras that use them. Although the instant-picture camera has been considered by many to be best suited to snapshots rather than professional-quality photographs, recent advances in optics and films have made instant cameras adaptable to a wide range of photographic situations. Many professional photographers load their medium-format cameras with Polaroid instant film (using a special attachment designed for this purpose); others use an instant camera to make test photographs before beginning to work with their other cameras.

So far, Kodak's PR-10 film and Polaroid's SX-70 film are limited to prints only: There is no negative film or slide film available. However, Polaroid does make a positive/negative film for some types of instant cameras. You can have an enlargement made from the Polaroid negative just as you would when using the negative from a non-instant camera. But if you wanted an enlargement made from a PR-1 or SX-70 print, you'd have to find a processing lab that would photograph the photograph. This can be expensive. In our view, the disadvantages of instant film outweigh the advantages in model photography.

Light and Color Film

The type of film you will use depends to a great degree on the type of light you will be using. Films differ in the way they record light.

Sunlight is considered the basis for all photography, just as it is for painting. Sunlight is rated in what is technically known as Kelvin temperature. Most color film is balanced for daylight; that is, for light in the range of 5,500 to over 6,000 degrees Kelvin. Light is considered warm (dominated by reds, oranges, and similar colors) when the degrees Kelvin are well below this range. Light is considered cool (dominated by blue, green, and similar shades) when it approaches the 6,000-degree figure. Noon sunlight is about 6,000 degrees Kelvin. The standard incandescent light such as you might use in a table lamp at home is 3,200 degrees Kelvin. Electronic flash and blue flashbulbs are meant for daylight color film used indoors. Photoflood bulbs, photographic incandescent bulbs, and clear flashbulbs are

One advantage to using a high-quality 35mm single-lens-reflex camera (1) involves the photographer's image--he looks like a pro. A far more significant benefit of owning a 35mm SLR is the ability to change lenses to suit the type of photograph desired. The camera's "normal" lens (2), used for full-figure work, can be removed and replaced with a telephoto for portraiture. Inexpensive instant cameras (3,4) are best suited to full-figure work. The same is true of most 35mm rangefinders (5) and viewfinders, which do not have interchangeable lenses.

meant for use with indoor color film used indoors. If you use daylight film inside with tungsten bulbs, the images will have a red or orange cast. If you use indoor film outdoors at noon, the images will seem too blue.

The combination of light and color film you use will determine the effectiveness of every photograph you take. It is essential that you become aware of all surrounding light (daylight coming through the window of a room for example). You should also notice objects that might reflect their light into the model's face, changing his flesh tone. For example, suppose you were to photograph a model in a park in late afternoon. The sunlight is fading and the sky is becoming reddish. If the model is in the open, his face will reflect the sun's warmth and the flesh tone will remain fairly natural. However, if you photograph the model under a tree, the light would be reflected from the green leaves of that tree. Instead of warm light striking the model's face, the flesh tone would be dominated by the cool colors of the surrounding foliage. The extra greenish light would give the model's skin a purple cast.

There are three types of color film sold for the four different types of lighting you are most likely to encounter. Daylight color film is meant for use in daylight and with other light that is strong in blue, such as that from electronic flash, blue flood bulbs, and blue flashbulbs and flashcubes. Indoor color film comes in two types. Type A is meant for use with photoflood bulbs and other light that has a Kelvin rating of 3,400 degrees. The Kelvin rating is found on the front of each bulb, so you do not have to worry about making a mistake. Type B film, also known as tungsten film, is meant to be used with tungsten photographic lighting equipment rated at 3,200 degrees. At this writing, Kodachrome Type A

is the only 3,400-degree film readily available, and it is sold only in 35mm size. Ektachrome, Agfachrome, and other films in sizes ranging from 35mm to 8 x 10 and larger are available in a variety of speeds for use with tungsten photographic lighting.

The only equipment needed for many types of outdoor photography is the correct film and a camera. So for now we'll concentrate on the types of indoor shooting that require special kinds of lighting equipment. We'll discuss indoor and outdoor "available light" photography in the Using All Kinds of Light chapter.

Photoflood, Tungsten, Quartz

The least expensive way to learn controlled lighting is through the use of photoflood or tungsten photographic bulbs and simple stands. These bulbs cost less than $2 each, are available in almost every camera store, and fit clamp holders that are available both in photography stores and the lighting sections of discount and hardware stores. Such bulbs have bases that screw into any socket, though their heat can be so intense that they are best not used with most types of household lamp holders. The 500-watt size is best to buy because it is the most versatile in terms of light output. Many photographers use three holders, each with a 500-watt photoflood or tungsten photographic light. Others prefer 1,000-watt bulbs.

Slightly more versatile and more expensive stands are available from photographic equipment dealers. Stands used by professionals are adjustable to ceiling height, and are sturdy enough to last for several years. They can run from seven to 10 times the price of the simple clamp holders.

All clamp holders should be purchased with reflectors which control the direction and intensity of the light.

Quartz lights, though extremely small, are more expensive than photoflood and tungsten photographic bulbs. A quartz light bulb can cost $20. The special stand for holding it can add as much as $200 to the total cost, depending upon the quality of the unit. The minimum price you pay for a holder, reflector, and stand is at least 10 times the cost of the clamp light used to hold the flood bulb.

Why use quartz lights if the expense is so great? There are several reasons. Normal flood bulbs and tungsten photographic equipment have a maximum life of six hours each, during which the bulbs darken. This darkening of the bulb changes the color temperature. If you photograph a model in color when a bulb is new, then use the identical pose and background illuminated by that same bulb after it has burned for four or five hours, the flesh tones in the two photos will differ slightly. Quartz lights have a normal life of up to 75 hours. The bulbs do not darken, so the same color temperature is given off throughout the bulb's life. These are the best lights to own for model photography handled on a regular basis; they should be avoided as long as you consider such work just an interesting hobby.

Electronic Flash

Electronic flash is the third type of direct lighting you can use with models in controlled settings. Unfortunately, electronic flash illuminates your subject for such a short time that it is impossible to predetermine the final effect just by flashing the unit while you watch the model. If you want to use electronic flash, you'll need what is known as a modeling light.

Professional-quality modeling lights are available in a wide range of prices. You can experiment with other types of makeshift modeling lights before investing in one of these.

Many types of electronic flash units have heads that can be adjusted to project light straight ahead (above, left), off the ceiling (center), and to the side (right). Bouncing the light can reduce or eliminate shadows (below).

The idea of a modeling light is to direct a continuous beam of light in the same direction as the light from the electronic flash. The goal is to determine how the light from the flash will strike the model. If a correctly positioned modeling light creates undesirable shadows or hot spots on the model, you can assume that the flash will also do so. You can use any small directional light source positioned near the flash unit to test for these unwanted shadows before you take your flash photograph.

Another problem with flash is determining the proper exposure. All floodlighted subjects can have the exposure determined by the meter built into your camera or by a hand-held light meter. Electronic flash requires either a lot of guessing, a special and very expensive light meter that can read the light striking the subject for just a fraction of a second, or an electronic flash unit that has a built-in automatic shutoff.

Electronic flash units that have built-in "eyes" designed to enable the flash to measure out a preselected amount of light and then shut off are called automatic flash units. If you wish to minimize the trial and error often required to get a good photograph using electronic flash, we believe you'll consider the added cost of an automatic flash a worthwhile investment.

Automatic flash units have many configurations. One type positions the electric eye and the light source on a single panel. Another type positions the light source on a movable head so that it can be turned away from the subject while the eye remains pointed at the subject. The latter configuration is by far the more versatile. By moving the head away from the model and bouncing the light off a wall or the ceiling, for example, you can eliminate shadows and other unwanted effects while softening the light in a pleasing way.

But if you do not wish to buy a movable-head-type flash, there are a few things you can do with an immovable-head type to soften the light it emits. For example, you can position a half-cylinder made of paper in front of the light element and fasten it there with tape. This diffuses the light. You can experiment (we would hope on your own, not with the model present) by using a variety of papers in front of the flash. There are special diffusors available for many types of electronic flash units. These are made of frosted plastic.

There are also special accessories designed for bouncing the light from a flash unit. These are called umbrella reflectors. An umbrella reflector is nothing more than an umbrella-type frame covered with a special cloth that is highly reflective. Most are silver, some are white, and some are gold-colored. (One manufacturer, Larson Reflectasol, offers a blue-colored reflector that converts light from a quartz or flood bulb to a color temperature matching daylight. This allows you to use daylight film in studio settings with lights normally rated for tungsten or Type A films.)

The umbrella is mounted on a stand so the light strikes the material and is reflected back toward the model. The light from an umbrella reflector differs from the light achieved when a flash is bounced off the ceiling or walls. An umbrella allows for more "sculpting" of facial and body details than is possible with light bounced off room surfaces. Equally important is the fact that the umbrella light is consistent in color temperature; the color of light bounced off the walls or ceiling is dependent on the color of the reflecting surface.

There are numerous inexpensive alternatives to the umbrella reflectors. For example, the simplest silvered reflector is made of aluminum foil. Take a large piece of corrugated card-board or other lightweight, stiff material and cover one side with the foil. If you want more diffused lighting effects, crinkle the foil in your hands before placing it on the cardboard. Aluminum foil can even be attached to a regular umbrella for use as a reflective surface. You can wrap either the inside or outside, then secure it with needle and thread. However, unlike the silvered umbrellas sold commercially, which can be closed and opened without damage, a homemade foil umbrella cannot be closed without tearing the foil. Rather than replacing the foil each time, leave your umbrella open.

White surfaces make excellent reflectors. This means white cards, a handkerchief, a sheet or anything else. You can sew a white sheet to a regular umbrella for an excellent reflector. You can also lay a handkerchief on the floor in front of a reclining model, keeping the material just out of camera range. This is especially effective for a model with deep-set eyes, since the cloth will reflect light onto her face. White walls are natural reflectors. You can take a portrait with the model leaning against the wall as though resting. It seems a natural pose and no one will ever realize you are using the reflective surface to add light.

The model's clothing can serve as a reflector. A white dress, white hat, white scarf or similar material can all add light to her face. If your model's outfit includes a white hat and the lighting is such that the face is shadowed, have the model hold the hat in her hand. Keep the hat near the model's face; the reflection from the texture surface will illuminate her.

Creating a Home Studio

Most photographers are misunderstood by their families or roommates. Refrigerators were meant to store film, yet some people erroneously believe that such devices are actually supposed to hold food, milk, and other nonessential items. These same deluded non-photographers believe that the large photography studio built into every home and apartment should be called a "living room." The typical home photography

The model's clothing can be used to reflect light onto her face. A white blouse or dress might help to reduce unwanted shadows on her skin.

studio is cluttered with furniture; a television set; and perhaps some family members, dogs, and other creatures. No one but you is likely to be aware of the true purpose of the room, and this can cause some problems.

The first step toward equipping a home photography studio is to lay it out in your head without telling anyone what you are doing. A space at least 10 feet wide will be needed to hold the seamless paper background, which is almost essential for your work. (Of course, the greater the area of your studio, the better.) An alternative to the paper is a smooth, white wall. This is good only for partial figure photography. Full-figure work requires you to step back far enough so that the floor will be visible. Any kind of floor will create an obvious break in the photograph and will draw attention away from your subject. Therefore, seamless paper is recommended. Seamless paper is inexpensive, available through most camera stores (sometimes by special order only), lightweight, and easily hung.

Ideally, you would use seamless paper stands—either the type which are free-standing, very much like portable light stands, or spring-loaded units which are held up by pressure against the floor and ceiling. Such commercial stands start at prices from $35 to $50 each and can go to several hundred dollars.

An alternative to the custom stand costs from $1 to $3. It includes two metal hooks and a length of nylon cord—that's all. The hooks screw into the ceiling at a distance no more than eight inches to a foot from either end of the paper roll. Take the nylon cord and drop it through the opening of the roll. Then tie that end to the first hook. It is easiest to make a knot in the rope, then slip the loop over the end of the hook. Raise the seamless paper roll to the ceiling, pull the other

Seamless paper enables the photographer to make the background of the photo "disappear."

end of the rope to make it taut, and tie that end to the other hook. This takes just a moment but may require two people. Unroll enough paper to reach the floor, then come forward five to seven feet. Since the paper has been rolled, it will tend to curl. Weight down the corners with books.

Before the model steps on the paper, he should carefully wipe the bottoms of his shoes on a cloth, rug or other surface you provide. Then he should place fresh masking tape on the bottoms of his shoes (don't let any tape show around the edge) to create a barrier between the shoes and the seamless paper. This slows the dirtying and

destruction of the paper. If the model is not going to be shown full-figure, ask him to slip off his shoes before stepping onto the paper.

When you finish your photography session, you can roll the paper up to the ceiling and out of the way, or slip the rope off the hooks and store the paper roll in a closet.

The floor on which you work is a consideration. Carpeting is a bad surface if you will be using female models who'll be wearing high heels. The points of the heels will break through your seamless paper. Using a room with a wood or tile floor is a help. If the only available room is carpeted, position a large sheet of plywood or other sturdy material between the carpet and the paper.

Many homes lack the wiring necessary to handle the load of 500-watt bulbs on any one circuit—especially when other items such as lamps, radio, and television are operated from the same line. Long, heavy-duty extension cords can be used to tap into additional circuits. (To learn where the different circuits might be, check your circuit-breaker box or fuse box.) Use long enough extension cords to assure adequate slack: A taut cord can pull a light off balance.

You'll probably have to move furniture around to clear a space large enough for modeling. The model might therefore see furniture stacked up everywhere, but that is not what will be recorded on film.

Eventually, as your skills increase and the results of your model photography sessions begin to attract a lot of praise around your household, you might be allowed to set up a room as your permanent studio. You'll be able to equip such a room with all of the unwieldy light stands, tripods, and props you want—without disturbing anyone. Until then, you'll be pleased to see how much you can accomplish in a temporary studio.

Finding Someone to Model

Now all you need is a subject. The person you'll photograph will be one of the following: a friend or relative, a stranger you meet by chance, or a professional model.

Family and Friends

You'll probably begin with someone you know. Perhaps your grandfather's wrinkles and ruddy complexion tell an intriguing story. Maybe you're dating a man who looks like he stepped out of the pages of *Gentlemen's Quarterly* magazine, or you're seeing a woman who could pose for *Vogue.* Your niece, your next-door neighbor, your husband or wife—all, no doubt, have faces that deserve to be photographed. Such models are readily available, and they know enough about you to not suspect you have an ulterior motive in asking them to pose. And such models are inexpensive: You won't have to pay them or even buy them a fancy dinner, since they'll probably consider your flattery reward enough.

But using family members and friends as models can present some problems. One is that they might be reluctant to put much time into the work. A friend might expect you to take no more than a half dozen shots before stopping so you both can go off and do something more

interesting. (You won't have the nerve to say that you bought four rolls of film for the session.) Trained models, on the other hand, are often willing to work for two, three or more hours, even when they're just getting free prints in exchange for posing. They often regard each session as a learning experience; each shot another chance to perfect their posing skills. Thus, they will endure uncomfortable situations—wearing a fur coat for hours indoors or a bathing suit outside in a blizzard.

Another problem in using family and friends is that you might forget to study their physical assets and liabilities as carefully as you would those of a stranger. You might find that you know your wife or husband too well to notice the little blemish that will ruin your portrait. You might concentrate on capturing your boyfriend's cute smile, and not realize that his eyes are bloodshot. No one really knows how many marriages, love affairs, and friendships have been shattered by the imperfect pictures that resulted from such first-time modeling sessions.

If you decide to work with friends or family, force yourself to be objective about the person's face, his expression, and the way the light strikes his features. Study your model

before looking through your camera and again while you are framing him in the viewfinder. Try to think of your friend as a stranger rather than allowing your familiarity with him to distort your vision. Look upon the person as a piece of sculpture or a study in light and shadows, not as an object of your affection.

A Chance Acquaintance

The person you meet on the street, in a restaurant, at a nightclub, in the office or somewhere else might be easier for you to photograph than a friend or family member because of your lack of emotional involvement. Such a person catches your eye because of his physical appearance. You don't know the individual's personality, so you can be objective about the way he looks. You will find it easy to spot unattractive details, which can be minimized with careful lighting. Unfortunately, while such a person is easier to photograph, mustering the nerve to request a pose is often difficult.

You ask yourself: "Will he think I'm flirting?" or "Will she think I'm trying to pick her up?" or "Will the old woman think I'm being cruel and mocking her appearance?" These questions and more are likely to go

When beginning to take posed pictures of people, many amateur photographers approach friends or relatives, perhaps those whose "character lines" tell an interesting story (1). When photographing such subjects, a photographer can sometimes fail to notice undesirable details like hair that looks a bit too windblown (2). A nearly perfect image (3) results when the photographer studies everything seen through the viewfinder.

through your mind as you try to decide how to approach the potential model.

Photographers who use casual acquaintances as models have found that the approach determines the reaction. Many people will be flattered by your interest, and assume you are sincere. Once they realize that all you want is a photograph, they either cooperate or walk away smiling. .

Before you approach a would-be model, have some business cards made. These cards should have the name of your studio, if any, or at least "John/Jane Doe Photography," and an address and telephone number where you can be reached during business hours. If you are normally home only in the evening, put the evening hours on your cards. Such cards give you an image of stability and make it clear that you are trying to show a degree of professionalism. Business cards are inexpensive. Even if you have no intention of earning money with your camera, they will not be a waste. They reassure potential models, and this can be extremely important.

If you don't carry business cards, you should carry paper on which you can write your name and number. Models must never be asked for their home addresses or telephone numbers. Such an approach sounds threatening to many people. You must allow your potential subjects to feel that they are in complete control of whatever happens. When they have your business card or even a sheet of paper on which you have written your name and telephone number, they know they can either contact you or not as they see fit. If they work with you, it will be because they took the initiative. This makes them more enthusiastic about posing for you.

Tell the person in whom you are interested exactly why you want to photograph her. Spot a good feature for photography,

one the person can see in a mirror, and explain that that feature is why you are interested. For example, you might say: "I am a photographer and I think you have a very beautiful face for photography. From any angle, I believe it would record in an interesting manner." Or you might say to an older person, "I am a photographer and am impressed by the depth of character in your face. I would like to take your picture and try to capture that quality on film." You might comment about the color of a woman's hair, the expressiveness of a man's eyes or whatever else seems appropriate. This tells the person that you truly have studied his or her appearance.

You will notice that each approach started with: "I am a photographer. . . ." Say this whether you own a simple, fixed-lens camera or expensive professional equipment. It creates a favorable impression. You'll be stating who you are and what you do. The fact that photography is your hobby rather than your profession is unimportant. Any other approach may sound too bold.

Ask the person to call you if he or she is interested in posing for you. Say that you would like

Perhaps it was the smile of a chance acquaintance that attracted the photographer. He should tell her so when he asks to take her picture.

to meet to discuss matters further and suggest a local coffee shop. Never ask the model to come to your home. A coffee shop is open to the public and "safe." It presents no risk.

During your meeting with the model, you'll need to show samples of your work. This is just as true when working with modeling agencies and modeling schools as it is when working with someone who's never modeled before. Ideally, these samples will be pictures of other men and/or women. However, you can show any photographs you have taken that are of high quality. This is something you can do whether your camera is simple or complex.

Sample prints can be any size larger than snapshots, although 8 x 10s are best. Color slides should be shown in a hand viewer (bring an extra bulb and spare batteries) for convenience. You can show scenics, street scenes, pictures of children or anything else you feel is effective. A professional photographer must show either some 8 x 10-inch or 11 x 14-inch prints. However, an amateur can use 4 x 5s or, preferably, 5 x 7s without problems. Your collection of photos is your portfolio.

The reason for the portfolio is to show the model and/or the agency that you are competent with a camera, even if you have never photographed a model. As we've said, casual acquaintances and friends will often pose simply because they are pleased that you like their looks. But experienced models and modeling students will want to be certain you are serious about photography and are more advanced than a snapshooter. They'll also be aware that you're just starting out in the field, but usually will not hold your lack of experience and/or equipment against you.

Modeling Agencies and Schools

After you've acquired some expertise and confidence, you

might decide to contact a modeling agency. The quality and services of such agencies vary around the country. Ideally, a modeling agency is a professional organization that represents men and women of all ages who are available to be photographed for advertisements, to appear in commercials, to present information at trade shows and conventions, and to model fashions. Professional models can earn a very good living in New York, Los Angeles, and other major markets. Smaller cities—such as Cleveland, Detroit, and San Francisco among others—form the middle markets. Here modeling opportunities are numerous, but most models have to supplement their income with part-time jobs. Still smaller communities are unlikely to have any full-time models; and if a man or woman can work one hour a week as a model in such a location, he or she is doing well.

All modeling agencies work with photographers on a fee basis. A model can be hired for use in a specific advertisement as well as to pose for a photographer's experimental projects. Photographers who want to update their portfolios often hire models or work out an exchange agreement: The model receives prints for *her* portfolio in exchange for posing without charge for the photographer's needs. The understanding usually is that the photographs being taken will not be sold, but will be used only as examples of the photographer's skills.

Modeling agencies always screen a photographer's request for a model, even when this is a trade arrangement of prints for posing. The agency heads want to be certain that the photographer is professional and legitimate. A surprising number of so-called photographers have highly questionable intentions. The agencies' screening process protects the models.

Modeling schools are likely to be interconnected with agencies, though some operate independently. The best modeling schools teach the students how to pose and how to use make-up, among other skills. The worst are little more than charm schools whose graduates have little or nothing of value to offer agency clients. The agency connection enables these substandard schools to attract new students ("After you pass our course, you will be registered with our agency so that you can begin your new career in the exciting world of...." *ad nauseum*). Few if any of the models registered with the agency will ever be placed in jobs, but the would-be models fail to realize this until after they've paid their tuition.

Large modeling agencies are a fine source of subjects if you are a professional photographer. Chances are that you're not a pro: You simply enjoy taking pictures of people and want to learn to do it better. You need someone to pose for you, but you lack the sophistication and equipment that would make you feel competent with a professional model. And you might not have the money to pay even the token fee some agencies charge. To an agency that charges $55 an hour for a model, a fee of $10 an hour or slightly more is a mere token; but to the average person with a camera, that $10 is a big expense, and money that could be better used for processing still-life photos.

Modeling schools and agencies in smaller communities are eager to give their models as much experience in front of a camera as they can. If you offer to give the model some duplicate prints for her portfolio, such places might be happy to let you photograph without charge.

All model portfolios measure either 8 x 10 inches or 11 x 14 inches. If business potential is limited, models carry several copies of their favorite 8 x 10 enlargement to hand to potential clients. The 8 x 10 is large enough to command attention, yet small enough to fit into a standard-size file folder. Models working in communities so large that giving out prints is not economically practical often have composites made. A composite is an 8 x 10-inch sheet of paper or a 16 x 10-inch sheet folded in half, printed on both sides by a commercial printing shop that works from photos or negatives. Such composites are made up of two or more photographs each and are purchased in quantities of 100 copies or more. Composites are cheaper for a model to make than duplicate photographs, except in very small quantities.

Any portfolio larger than 11 x 14 loses impact because the pictures are difficult to study. (Back in the late 1950s and early 1960s, advertising agencies were in their glory. Corporate advertising budgets were big, and many large agencies were making even bigger profits. The art directors and account executives who hired photographers usually had giant offices. They could examine oversized portfolios by propping them against a wall and stepping back to look. Then a severe recession hit the industry, forcing everyone to retrench. Budgets were cut and most agencies reduced their floor space. No longer was there space available to step back from a 16 x 20 portfolio in order to study it. And so, since 11 x 14 prints can be seen easily from normal viewing distances when set on a desk, this became the standard maximum in the field.)

We've told you about the cameras, lighting equipment, business cards, and sample photographs you'll need to get started in model photography. You might be lacking another important ingredient: the nerve to ask a stranger or a professional model to pose for you. Go ahead and ask. The worst anyone can do is say no.

Working with the Model

You're ready to take the first few shots of your first-ever modeling session. Your nonprofessional model stands in front of your camera, smiles, and asks, "What would you like me to do?" Your hands begin to sweat, you stammer, and in your panic you realize that you don't have the slightest idea. The person who has agreed to pose for you is doing you a favor and is looking to you for guidance, but you don't know what to say. "All right," you begin, "I want you to look, um, well, natural." Your model stares at you blankly.

So you take the trial-and-error approach, experimenting with poses. Some are mildly interesting; most are awkward. You run a lot of film through your camera, and the ratio of good shots to bad ones is far too low.

A professional model might have been able to help you a bit, but even a pro would have relied on you for some direction. Posing techniques are the same whether the model is an amateur or a professional, because the model's fee or lack of one has nothing to do with what makes someone look "right" in a photograph. Your ability to portray on film what it was about your model that first attracted you to him or her depends on several factors. Among them are the model's interest in what you're doing, and your understanding of some basic posing techniques.

We'll begin with a discussion of the types of model photography that can be done with low-priced 110-format cameras, 126-formats, or 35mm viewfinders and rangefinders which generally have wide-angle lenses. At the end of this chapter, we'll center in on portraiture, which often requires lenses having longer focal lengths than the lenses of most inexpensive cameras.

Preparing for the Session

A beginning model can be guided by the poses other models have found effective. Before your model photography session, thumb through fashion magazines and general-interest publications. Look at the advertisements and the illustrations, cutting out any that have strong appeal. You can mount these clippings in a scrapbook or place them in a box. Have your model study the poses, and let her imitate some of them.

Carefully frame the model in the viewfinder. Studio settings enable you to isolate the model against a continuous backdrop, so there is little to worry about other than the angle, facial expression, and appearance of the clothing. When you are on location, however, you will need to study the model in relation to the surroundings. Can she be framed by trees and rocks? Can she be positioned against a doorway? One angle might place her in such a relationship to telephone poles that one seems to be growing out of her head; a slight shift in position might make for a perfect picture.

Check the corners of the frame to see what surprises might be lurking in the background. A red object at the edge of the frame of a color photo will draw the viewer's eye away from the model. Warm colors such as red and orange should appear in the picture only where they will enhance the main subject. A model wearing a red blouse should also wear a red ribbon, scarf or hat to draw the viewer's eye to her face. Cool colors—objects that are blue, green, and the like—seem to fade into the distance.

Advertising photographers frequently take advantage of their knowledge of how colors are perceived. Suppose a model is standing next to some products. If the model is to be emphasized, she will usually wear warm colors when the product is a cool color. The reverse color scheme is used when the model is less important than the products.

The posing should fit the clothing. A model wearing tennis togs will not hold herself the same way she would if she were wearing an evening gown. A sports outfit can be shown more effectively with a wide stance and body movement; the formal clothing lends itself to more controlled positions.

The model should bring her own clothing to the session. This clothing should be carried separately rather than worn to the photography location. Clothing worn while traveling to the site or studio will likely be wrinkled.

Solid colors are best when you are first learning to pose a model. Patterned fabrics may

The model stares into the camera (1) and asks, "What would you like me to do?" The photographer should be able to provide some guidance. Prior to the session, the photographer should explain what types of clothing might work best. Patterned fabrics (2) can conflict with the scenery. Clothing should be carried to, not worn to, the session. This helps to avoid unattractive wrinkles in the fabric (3).

conflict with the designs of props and chairs. They might also confuse the eye of the viewer.

Most models you use will bring clothing that may not fit them quite right. If you use a professional model, she may have her own wardrobe or, more likely, she will use clothing from a boutique, department store or other source where she has connections. These items of apparel are usually "off the rack," so even the selection of an appropriately sized garment is no assurance of the perfect fit needed for the clothing to record most effectively. An amateur might panic after agreeing to pose for you, and run around trying to borrow a blouse from one friend, a skirt from another, and a tennis outfit from a third. All the outfits will come close to fitting, but none will be exactly right. The result is that a model with a beautiful figure might wear an outfit that makes her look slightly overweight. Material needs to be pinched here, pulled there, and otherwise altered. Fortunately, this can be easily done. Professionals handle the matter with spring-clip clothespins. Ask the model to alter her outfits by clipping the material where the clips will not be visible. This usually means clipping the clothing behind her back or to one side.

Make-up can be applied anywhere, provided the model has a chance to touch up just before being photographed. This may mean that the photographer will have to carry a mirror in the car or make sure a clean restroom is available. Make-up is a potential danger to the model's clothing. The model should take a chiffon scarf, place one end between her teeth, drape the body of the scarf over her head, and then pull the clothing over her head. This protects the clothing from her make-up, and the scarf is so thin that it will not disrupt her hair. The same trick should be used when clothing is removed.

The model should have to do as little preparation on location as possible. Her make-up should be fairly complete when she arrives and she should be able to move into position with a change of clothing. Most male models will not wear make-up, though some may use a small amount to hide a scar or other disfiguring mark.

Choosing a Location

The site chosen for the photography session can have a great effect on the composition of the pictures and the way the model relates to you and your camera. For your first few experimental sessions with a model, we recommend an outdoor setting.

Most beginning models will be more comfortable working with you on location than they'd be in your home. If you are male and the model is female, or the other way around, working on location might seem less threatening to both of you. Outdoors there are enough distractions to alleviate nervousness. A model may feel very relaxed romping in a park while you take photographs, even though you have never worked together before and she has never posed for anyone. Place that model in front of an indoor backdrop and special lights, and she might become quite nervous. The work is the same, but the controlled studio-type surroundings are so unfamiliar that the subject's full attention is focused on having her picture taken. Thus it will be difficult for her to be "natural." Your opportunity to capture a sort of candid-posed shot will be better outdoors.

It is best to have your locations spotted in advance rather than to work randomly. You might want to spend an hour in an urban setting, and another hour or two in a park. You certainly should not expect your model to drive around with you while you search for a visually

1

interesting site. If you find yourself doing much location work with models, you might try a trick used by professionals. Keep your camera handy when you travel around your community and nearby areas. Each time you see an interesting location, snap a picture of it and make note of the spot. You might make a file of contact prints pasted onto 3 x 5 cards on which you can write a full description of the site.

When working outside, encourage a model to relate to the surroundings. Have the model touch a low-hanging branch of a tree or pick a flower. Let her run through a field or lean against a tree. Have her stand on a hill with the breeze blowing through her hair and her head silhouetted against the sun or backlighted by the harsh light.

A model probably will find a way to apply her make-up almost anywhere (1),but the photographer should plan ahead to make this as convenient as possible. Location sessions can be conducted indoors at a place of business (2), or outdoors (3). The photographer should plan ahead here, too, so he and the model can go quickly to the photography site.

Try framing the model with trees, rocks, and other items. Then have her move around in the frame while you look for the right angle.

Not all location shooting must be done outdoors, of course. You might try to arrange for a session inside a building. Remember that all buildings, including an enclosed mall, are technically private property. You can be asked to leave, so try to remain as inconspicuous as possible.

Some locations will delight in your using their facilities if you ask at times when you will not disturb anyone. These places include resorts during the off-season, restaurants an hour or more before opening, some museums prior to opening, art galleries, and other locations that view your work as capable of providing publicity for them. Even if you're a beginner, many such businesses will allow you to work on their grounds. Just be certain you do not interfere with the staff or guests and that you pick up all trash and personal belongings. Film wrappers, boxes, and other junk left behind will not be appreciated.

If you want to use a specific business as a location, contact the manager's office, president's office, public relations department, etc. The specific business will determine who you should call.

After you've acquired some experience in working with a model, and she's had time to get to know you well enough to feel comfortable in your presence, you might want to move into your home studio. An indoor setting will increase your control over such factors as lighting and poses, and eliminate such things as high winds which can destroy the mood of the pictures you want. A studio-type site will also enable you to provide some items that will be useful to the model.

A large mirror propped behind the camera can be of help. As the poses change, the model can take a more active role in correcting small problems such as hair out of place or a hand positioned awkwardly. Be alert to the model who uses the mirror as a crutch, however. Some models will study themselves and completely ignore you and the camera. When this happens, lay the mirror down or turn it aside.

One popular way to help a model relax is the use of music. Turn on a portable radio or your stereo system. Let the model pick the station or choose a record or tape from your collection, and adjust the volume to the level she finds most enjoyable. If you decide to take model photographs on a regular basis, you might want to buy record albums or tapes covering everything from country music to jazz to classical in order to suit the tastes of the models you use.

Full-Figure Poses

We'll assume for a moment that you'll be taking full-figure photographs rather than close-ups. If you have a camera with a fixed, slightly wide-angle lens, you'll have little choice, since such a lens tends to exaggerate perspective at close range and increase the perceived size of a person's nose, for instance. Actually, full-figure composition is the way most model photography work is handled, even by professional photographers. Usually they work with fashions, so the model is either standing, sitting, kneeling or reclining—all poses that can be recorded effectively with any kind of camera.

Standing. The simplest approach to standing poses is called the clock method. Your model stands with her weight on her left foot, and the toes of that foot pointed away from her right foot, at a 45-degree angle from the camera's line of "sight." The left foot should be imagined to be at the center of a clock face.

The clothing will affect the pose. A tennis outfit, for example, will allow the model to assume a wide stance which would not be appropriate if formal clothing were worn.

The second, "free" foot is going to be the "hand" of the clock, pointing to each hour. The model will start posing by placing her free foot so that the toe is aimed towards the camera (noon position). The ankle should be slightly bent. Then the free foot is moved to the one o'clock position, the two o'clock position, and so forth. This can be reversed, with the right foot at the center of the clock and the left foot moving from 12 to 11 to 10. In addition to the foot movement, the model should try to keep her shoulders parallel to the floor. Her hips will be twisted slightly away from the

camera at much the same angle as the weight-bearing foot.

There are numerous posing variations that can be brought into play for different types of outfits. A casual pose, perhaps with the model wearing a tennis or jogging outfit, might have her standing with her feet apart, toes pointing outward, and her weight evenly distributed. The shoulders remain parallel to the floor as she leans from side to side, varying the position of her hands. She might tilt her head to the left and lean so the right leg moves out in the opposite direction. She can also vary her position by twisting her body slightly to the right or left.

Nobody's perfect. The most gorgeous or handsome model you've ever seen in a magazine advertisement might not look nearly so attractive in person. The reason is that the photographer no doubt spent a great deal of time in finding the best possible angle and arranging the light exactly right, and used up many rolls of film to capture the model at his or her very best. On the street, that model might look far too skinny or a bit too plump to you, and have more wrinkles than you saw in the ad or a facial feature that looks good only from one angle.

We're assuming now that you're going to be trying for glamour photos, not character studies. So we'll discuss some aspects of a model's appearance that would be considered as imperfections only in terms of fashion and glamour photography.

Your model's legs might be too thin or too heavy. Her waist might need slimming. Perhaps her nose, nice as it is, seems a bit too long. You certainly won't be able to rearrange the model's features, but you will be able to de-emphasize those that are less than perfect.

You might be working with a model who is as near to perfect as anyone can be, yet you consistently get photos that make her look unattractive—even ugly. Some distortion can be caused by the camera lens. It can be especially bothersome to users of cameras having non-interchangeable lenses, which are slight wide-angles.

The problem results from a hand, foot or other portion of the model's body being closer to the lens than some other feature. Perhaps you've seen wide-angle photographs of a baseball pitcher warming up for the throw. His foot is in the air and the camera is positioned near it with a wide lens. The foot appears extremely large, dwarfing the head and throwing arm. This distortion usually occurs with close-ups, but can happen in full-figure photography as well. To avoid it, try to keep all parts of the model's body on the same plane. To reduce the chances of such distortion, many photographers rely on longer lenses; that is, telephotos. These magnify the image and compress perspective, often with very pleasing results. For example, a long lens used for portraiture can foreshorten the model's long nose.

Even if you can't change your lens, you can change your angle, thereby compensating for the shortcomings of your equipment and some imperfections in the model's anatomy.

Suppose your model is somewhat heavy and her waist appears a little thick. Have her turn so that her head is facing you but her body is in profile. Ask her to inhale deeply, exhale to relax, then inhale again as you take the picture. This flattens the stomach.

Have a standing model slowly turn around as you watch. Even a model who looks attractive when standing facing the camera—and few do—will look more attractive as she turns. A full-front picture is seldom complimentary to a model who has slightly heavy legs. Have the model make a half turn of her body. The leg closest to you should be placed slightly forward, with the foot pointed so

the sole of the foot is arched. This can make the legs look slimmer.

Taking pictures from a high angle helps to eliminate a too-thin appearance. But the high angle has to be used with care. If you position your camera too high in relation to the model, especially if she is sitting, her legs may seem too small (the result of the distortion we discussed earlier). Lower angles are usually more effective when emphasizing attractive legs.

Sitting. Body angle can be critical when the model is sitting. The model may have her legs together and stretched out to one side or together and bent at the knees. In the latter pose, the model's feet should be pointed in the same direction as the knee-to-ankle line. If the model crosses her legs, shift your position relative to her. Work both high and low, walking around her. Note how the legs become either a design element or slightly obtrusive depending on where you stand. A model should not cross her legs at the

knee, but as much above the knee as possible.

Leg position can be a problem when you shoot from a high angle. Often the legs of a sitting model will appear almost triangular: big at the knees; the feet seeming to disappear into the ground. For best effect, the model should angle her legs about 30 degrees away from the camera, with her feet positioned slightly in back of her knees as you shoot from a low position.

Few models can tuck their legs underneath themselves when seated and look attractive to the camera. However, you might find that this technique is best when working with a model whose legs are especially thin or thick: It effectively hides the legs completely.

You might also have a bit of trouble in photographing a sitting model from the waist up. She can look too thick-waisted, too broad-shouldered or otherwise out of proportion, depending on the camera angle. Experiment with a variety of camera positions. You can also ask her

The angle of camera to subject can be critical when sitting poses are used. A slight change in angle could exaggerate the model's legs in an unattractive manner.

to swing her arms and shoulders back a bit while she sits. This helps to reduce the unattractive effect of protruding collarbones.

Kneeling. The most effective poses for kneeling are similar to those for standing, in that the model is positioned at an angle to the camera for the most attractive look. The model might be kneeling with her body erect with her hands resting on her hips, or she might lower herself so that her bottom rests on her ankles and her hands rest on her knees.

Some model photographers like to have their models use a kneeling variation of the clock position for posing. The model kneels on one leg, letting that knee bear the body weight. The other leg is bent at a right angle or similarly graceful position, with the foot flat on the floor. The free leg is then moved towards the different numbers of the imaginary clock. This is then reversed so the weight-bearing leg becomes the free one. The foot of the free leg should always point towards the camera as much as possible.

Kneeling poses are the least comfortable for the model. It is the photographer's obligation to remain aware of this. Most photographers recognize the difficulty when the model is outdoors, kneeling in dirt and gravel. But they sometimes forget that kneeling even on carpeting for a short period of time can be painful.

Reclining. A reclining model can be extremely attractive, whether photographed from her level or from above. You can lie on the floor across from her, use a waist-level finder, or stand so that you are looking down from above.

One problem with the reclining-model photograph is the way in which the model's body weight is distributed. A model resting on her arm will have an exaggerated shoulder, so the model's weight should actually be supported by her spinal column. The arms may look as though they are supporting weight, but should someone knock an arm out of the way, the model's position would not change because the weight is really distributed along her spine.

There are no general right and wrong ways to pose a reclining model, because everything depends on the model's angle to you. As long as she looks attractive when you study her image in the viewfinder, the photograph will be good.

Wide-angle lenses are sometimes desirable when photographing reclining models. Unfortunately, the use of such lenses increases the chance for the distortion mentioned earlier. Be certain the model is photographed on a plane parallel to the camera if you use such a lens.

Arm and hand placement. The placement of arms and hands is important in the shaping of the full-figure model. Have the model place one hand on her waist and see what the effect will be. Ask her to brush a lock of hair from her forehead or toy with her jewelry. Your model's hands should always be relaxed. The back of the hand is usually the hand's least attractive feature. If you must show the back of a model's hands, suggest an exercise that is used by

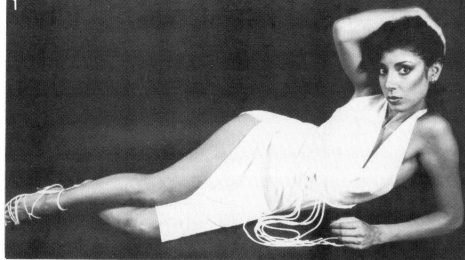

professional hand models. They hold their hands up near their shoulders, with their wrists limp, and shake their hands lightly. This shaking continues until it is time to pose for the picture, and is repeated as necessary. It changes the blood flow so the veins do not stand out on the back of the hands.

Normally, the wrists should be slightly flexed and the hands shown from the side. The elbows should be curved rather than rigidly bent. This makes for a more relaxed, natural appearance.

The Moving Model

Whether you do your photography indoors or out, you may decide to try some action shots. Fast movement can be handled with all kinds of cameras if you plan carefully.

The best way to handle movement, especially with a simple camera, is to watch for the high

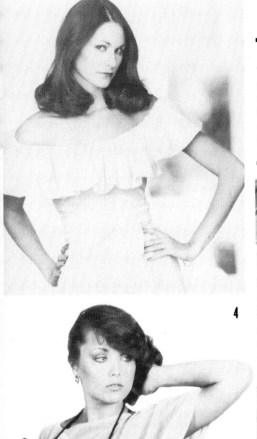

3

4

The position of the model's head, arms, and legs is very important. When asking for a reclining pose (1, 2), the photographer should remain aware of the way the model's body weight is distributed. The model can change the feeling of the image with a slight adjustment of her hands and arms (3, 4). When photographing a moving model, a photographer can catch the instant of peak action, such as the point at which the model turns, then stops her head and faces the camera (5).

5

point of an action. There sometimes is an instant during rapid action when a model is actually standing still. For example, suppose a model leaps into the air. When the model reaches the high point of the leap, just before she starts dropping back to earth, the model is actually not moving at all. By anticipating the high point, you can take a photograph that conveys all the excitement of motion with a camera that lacks very high shutter speeds.

You do not have to limit yourself to leaps. Peak action exists in many situations. If a model twirls, then stops and turns her head toward the camera, her head will be still while her hair and clothing continue to move. A dancer will also have numerous brief moments when action effectively stops. (This is especially true of ballet at moments when the ballerina is lifted by her partner.)

A leaping model is best recorded from an angle allowing you to look up at her. This means that your backdrop must be much higher than the typical home ceiling will allow. You can also effectively record a leap by using a small stepladder and standing so that you are looking down on the model. If you use seamless paper (a continuous paper roll which photographs as a solid color) for the background, the high angle shot will be effective. If you were to take the picture from a normal angle, your camera would capture part of the ceiling and all the background equipment, detracting from the final image.

Action posing can be handled even when working in a small space. Outdoors, you might have the model walk toward you or move across your field of vision. Indoors, instead of walking, have her rock back and forth, with her feet positioned as though she were actually moving forward. This keeps her on a fairly even plane and allows you to convey the effect of movement without having to adjust your own position or refocus the lens.

Some professional photographers use wind machines to add to the illusion of movement. They blow a stream of air at the model's hair and, at times, her clothing. This helps give a feeling of excitement to the picture.

To suggest motion, the model can assume a walking pose and then rock back and forth.

You can duplicate this feeling at a fraction of the cost of a wind machine. Go to your neighborhood discount store and buy a fan. It doesn't have to be a big one: A simple one-speed unit, which you can position at whatever angle you want, is fine.

Taking Portraits

Portrait work involving just the model's head or head and shoulders is usually not effective with very simple cameras. Even many viewfinder/ rangefinder cameras having fixed lenses will not allow you to get close enough for truly tight work.

The closer the lens of such a camera is held to the face, the more apparent distortion you see. As you move to within a few inches from the face, certain features seem to become exaggerated, depending upon your angle. The nose might seem to grow longer, an ear might seem to enlarge, and the image will generally change from pleasing to grotesque.

The ideal lens for head-and-shoulder portraits is one that is longer than "normal"; that is, longer than 50mm for a 35mm SLR. Most photographers prefer a lens in the 85mm to 105mm range for the 35mm camera; some use a long 135mm lens. The lens should be able to focus close enough so the subject's head fills the frame at the minimum focusing distance of the lens. The effect is one of intimacy, without the distortion that would be caused by a normal or wide-angle lens held close enough to the subject to achieve a similar perspective.

This effect of intimacy can be troubling, especially if the photographer is of one sex and the model is of the other. A male photographer may be attracted to the model's mouth because, as he looks through the lens of his SLR, he feels as close to her face as he would be if he were physically positioned to kiss her. Such a situation can be un-

Some photographers become disturbed by the effect of intimacy when viewing a model's face through a telephoto lens.

A picture of a round face photographed at eye level is usually not flattering; a low camera angle exaggerates the roundness. High angles, especially with the head turned slightly, usually result in the best effects. The high angle works against you when photographing a long face. However, a straight-on camera angle usually works perfectly, especially when the subject looks directly into the camera instead of turning his head to the side. The oval face requires an eye-level view for a good effect. If the camera is slightly higher than eye level and the model's head is turned to the side, the image generally improves. A low angle is uncomplimentary to almost every model.

The model's eyes determine the type of photograph you will achieve. Eye contact with the viewer of the photograph can add an intimacy that will be lacking if the model's eyes are diverted from the camera. (Many photographers working with color film like to focus on the eyes of a female model for intimacy and on her lips for sensuality. The technique of focusing on

nerving if you are not prepared for it. Furthermore, a professional model can alter her expressions on cue and assume highly alluring looks one after the other without giving thought to the photographer, who may tend to take such looks personally. This can be so distracting that the photographs will suffer. A female photographer might be so attracted to her male model's eyes that she forgets to look at his hair, which is badly in need of combing.

In portrait photography, the photographer must try to see every component of the picture. How is the model's hair arranged? What about his facial type? Does he have an oval face, a long face or a round face? Are there scars or blemishes that should be de-emphasized? All elements of the photograph must be observed, analyzed, and changed should that prove necessary.

Before photographing anyone's face, study it carefully from all angles. Look at the left profile, then the right, and finally study the face head-on. You'll probably see what appears to be three distinctly different individuals. For some people, every change of a few degrees in facial angle results in a completely different look.

Facial types can make a difference in the angle you select.

The photographer should request various head positions (above) because they can greatly affect the model's appearance. Eye contact with the camera or the lack of it (below) can also change the mood of the picture.

the eyes of men is equally effective.) The camera's relationship to the angle of a model's head determines whether the eyes will seem to be wide or narrow. Stand in front of a mirror and look at a specific spot; raise your head slowly while watching that spot; then lower your head. Notice how the size of your eyes seem to increase and decrease as you move. The same effect can be seen through the camera. Thus, if you want the model's eyes to appear fairly large, ask him to lower his head in relation to the position of the lens.

Many beginning models have difficulty changing their expressions. You want to try to obtain a full range of emotions. This may require some psychological games. One approach is to have the model close his eyes and imagine a situation that can evoke the kind of expression you are seeking. He might think about a peaceful mountain scene. Such an image can result in an expression of serenity. Anger might be invoked by thinking about a fight with his boss or a close friend. Sadness can be induced by thinking about the death of a loved one or some other tragic loss. The person might think about disco dancing for one mood, a wild ride down a roller coaster for another. The model becomes an active participant in determining the emotion to be expressed.

An alternative approach is to talk with the model—something that many photographers find difficult to do. You can tell jokes or describe incidents meant to evoke a particular reaction. (At the extreme are the professionals who actually yell and scream at their models to anger them or drive them to tears. They get results, but most people hate to work with them.)

Facial expressions change in subtle ways. A model who is smiling with his lips together may look quite different when he relaxes his lips and lets his teeth show. Take pictures of each variation of a pose and study the prints or slides.

A skilled model can rapidly change expressions to give the photographer a wide range of moods to choose from. A skilled photographer can help an inexperienced model to create various emotions by using music, and perhaps by instructing the model to recall memories of sad times and happy times.

The hands are often as important in portraits (1) as they are in full-figure poses. It's wise to experiment with several different hand positions. The mood of the photo can also be affected by the way the model uses her hair. A model with long hair can change her appearance greatly by letting it hang down and then putting it up (2, 3).

Color films can bring out special effects with close-ups. A film such as Kodachrome which records red intensely can provide a startlingly sensual image. For example, have a female model nibble on a cherry, strawberry or a red lollipop. Be

certain that she moistens her lips first. You may want to add a glistening effect to the fruit or candy by spraying it with water.

The hands again come into play when taking close-ups of a model's face. A woman might bring one finger to her lip or bite on a fingernail. She might toy with her necklace or a lock of her hair. Men and women can pose with chin in hands or the chin leaning on just one hand. They can touch a hat or other head covering.

A model with long hair can change the shape of her face by the way she allows her hair to fall. She can let it hang evenly over her shoulders or throw it behind one shoulder and let it cascade over the other. The long hair can be used to partially hide one eye or completely block half the face. Have the model turn her head quickly, letting her hair fly. Take the picture when her hair is in motion, even if that means it will be slightly blurred.

Don't Touch!

During such poses, you might find verbal instructions almost impossible; you'll certainly find them time-consuming and frustrating. You'll be tempted to physically involve yourself when helping the model to pose. You'll want to use your hand to alter a lock of hair, turn the face

to just the right angle or otherwise touch the model in a way that doesn't seem to matter very much. Don't do it!

Always *tell* the model what changes in pose you want her to make. This shows a respect that keeps every modeling session on a professional level. Touching someone during a modeling session should be considered taboo. It is unprofessional and can be threatening. The model could become so uncomfortable after such physical contact that she will be too tense to pose effectively.

One little touch could destroy a rapport which had developed gradually over a period of many sessions. You won't want to do anything to build new walls between the model and you. In fact, your goal should be to break down walls. To do that, you'll have to use a bit of psychology. As you have the model move from position to position, speak encouragingly. When the model looks attractive, say so. Struggle with the model to find the perfect pose, and be ready with praise when it is found. A sense of teamwork will probably develop. This will give the model confidence and a desire to pose for you in the future; it will give you a feeling of accomplishment and professionalism; and it will improve your photographs.

Using All Kinds of Light

In a previous chapter, we discussed the various systems used by photographers to direct artificial light onto their subjects. In this chapter, we'll tell you how to use all kinds of light—sunlight, artificial "available" light, and light from photographic lighting systems—to your best advantage.

Available-Light Candids

It's very likely that your first photograph of a person you didn't know was a candid one, and that your subject to this day doesn't know you took the picture. It's fun to go out people-watching with a camera, and from each candid photo, you can pick up skills that will come in handy when you decide to ask someone to pose for you.

Indoor candids require films that are capable of being used in low-light conditions. Films rated at ASA 400 and above are often responsive enough to low light to be used indoors without flash. We think it's probable that you'll find more opportunities for candid "people" photography outdoors.

So long as the light is even, street candids are no problem. You can work quickly, focusing and taking the picture before your subject notices you. However, when the light is changing, such as bright sunlight and dark shadows between buildings, you'll need to work differently. At such times, you should estimate the person's path and direction, go to the area that offers the best light, and take your light reading; then focus on an imaginary point near that location and wait for your subject to approach. When your subject reaches the spot you've focused on, take the picture.

Some cameras do not have built-in light meters, which allow you to take a reading through the lens. With such a camera you should use either a hand, held meter or one attached to the outside of the camera. No matter what kind of meter you use, you might run into a few problems. You could be standing in the bright sunlight while your subject is in the shade and the meter would read for your location; your exposure probably would be incorrect. You can't simply walk over to the person to get a more accurate reading, because he or she might become annoyed.

One answer is to take your light meter reading from the palm of your hand. Angle your hand so that the underside is as shaded as the area where your candid subject is standing. Then read this darker area. Remember to compensate for flesh tone differences. If you are dark and the subject is light, decrease your exposure by at least one f-stop. If the subject is dark and you are light, you may need to increase your exposure slightly.

Sometimes your subject will be moving too rapidly for the shutter speed that the available light will allow you to use. There are two ways to compensate for this. The first is to reposition yourself so the subject is moving directly towards you. The apparent movement of someone walking towards you is always less than when the subject is walking across your field of vision. The second approach is to pan your camera. Focus on the subject, then move with the subject as you squeeze the shutter release. Watch the subject in your viewfinder and always try to keep the person at the same spot. Continue panning even after you hear the click of the camera. After two or three tries, you will master this procedure. The panning results in the subject being in sharp focus and the background being slightly blurred. Panning is an effective technique with any camera.

Sometimes you need to have a longer exposure than a simple point-and-shoot camera can normally give you. Many of the simplest cameras are still able to provide two different shutter speeds. One is the normal daylight exposure (often 1/90 second). The second, much slower (often 1/40 second), is meant for use with flashcubes. The flashcube light is fast enough to stop action, so the slower shutter speed does not present a problem. What most owners of such cameras fail to realize is that the flashcube setting can be used for available-light work. Take a fully used flashcube and insert it in the

Photographers who own a simple camera and no lighting equipment can easily take pictures of people outdoors (1). Many beginning photographers start with candid shots which require little or no interaction with the subject (2, 3). It is possible for a photographer to appear so uninterested in his subjects that they forget about the photographer's presence. This results in natural poses.

flash socket just as though you were going to take flash photographs with a working cube. Then use the camera normally in the low-light situation. No flash will disrupt the image, but the dead cube will switch the camera to the slower shutter speed. Thus you will have gained one of the benefits of an adjustable camera without owning one.

Flash is best avoided for candid work because it calls attention to what you are doing. Candid photography is most effective when it captures the mood of the people and the surroundings as they exist without your intrusion. A flash can add shadows and other distracting visual elements, not to mention hostility. Some people may not want you to take their photographs. You may know that they are not in the picture, but if they see the flash, they might become angry. Since even inexpensive electronic flash units tend to emit light in a fairly wide beam, someone far away from what you are seeing in the viewfinder could still think you have taken his or her picture.

Sometimes people become aware of and uneasy about your camera while you try to take pictures. So a good technique is to pretend that you are *not* interested in them. Look past them, holding your camera away from your eye; then study the scene in your viewfinder, looking past them again. If this ruse works, you will soon see the person looking back over his shoulder each time you lower the camera. The subject will have become convinced that he is not the subject of your interest.

An alternative is to use hand signals with the person. As the person begins to seem uncomfortable, motion to him as though you want him to move back just enough so he is not in the picture. Then, when he's perfectly framed but thinks he is just out of the image, take the picture.

Does this sound deceitful? Perhaps; yet we see little difference between merely watching an interesting person and taking that person's photograph—provided, of course, that you will not use the resulting photo in any way that would prove embarrassing or annoying to the subject. Most candid photography has as its subjects people who don't mind having their pictures taken but feel uncomfortable about having been singled out. By seeming as though you are taking a picture of someone or something else, you'll be able to allow your subject to relax.

Never be satisfied with getting just a candid photograph. There is an initial enjoyment in taking a picture of an interesting old man, a pretty girl, a rugged construction worker or almost anyone else who strikes your eye. However, if you wish to learn from your photos, you should plan these pictures as well as you can. Keep alert to ways to frame the person. Be aware of the colors around you and the way you might alter your image. Look for interesting framing devices. Take pictures through spoked wheels; at low angles; framed with flowers, trees, and other foliage.

Many photographers shun street photography because they worry about getting a model release. Releases are covered in detail later in this book. Our advice for now is to take the picture first and ask for the release later. Such releases are often unnecessary. As long as the pictures are sold as an example of your work, a release is seldom if ever needed. It is better to take an image and only be able to display it on your wall than to avoid taking a picture. Each photograph you take brings you closer to fully developing your skills. You need all the experience you can get, and working candidly on the street is a definite help.

Remember that lighting is the key to good candid photo-graphs. By keeping aware of how the sunlight is affecting your subject, you will be able to take top-quality photographs anywhere you go.

Sunlight and a Model

As we said earlier, an outdoor location might prove to be the most comfortable for you and for a model who'll be working with you for the first time. Unfortunately, you'll be working with a light source that you cannot control.

Though you will not be able to change the position of the sun in the sky, you can change the position of your model to allow the sunlight to fall on him in the most complimentary way. You can easily pose your model with the sun behind, in front or to the side. If you use a very simple camera, photographing with the sun directly in back of the model will be a matter of trial and error; an advanced camera will let you control the exposure of the model's face accurately.

Sunlight on days when the sky is clear can be very harsh, creating very bright and very dark spots. Some photographers prefer to work with models outside on overcast days, since clouds diffuse and soften the light. Others soften the sunlight themselves by using various techniques.

Many photographers create bounce lighting with buildings serving as the reflector. They position a model at such an angle that the building is in the direct sun and the model is in a shadowed area next to the portion of the wall that is receiving the harsh light. The intense light bounces off the wall and illuminates the model. The light is softened in a manner almost identical with what you would obtain from a large umbrella reflector, though you will have little control over the angle of the bounce. Some photographers will go so far as to set an umbrella reflector on a stand on the opposite side of the model to further control the light. The model stands so the wall receiving the sun reflects light against his right profile. The umbrella reflector is positioned so it catches the same light, then throws it against his left profile. A handmade reflector will work just as well as a store-bought umbrella. This is a lighting trick you can use with simple as well as sophisticated cameras.

When using color film, remember that the colors of the surrounding foliage are often reflected onto the model's face, causing an unnatural flesh tone to be recorded. Green grass can make the model look slightly purple. The same is true of the colors of tree leaves. This color change is visible to the eye if you choose to look for it. Many photographers make unwise assumptions when working outdoors. If the overall scene looks right to them, they see no reason not to take the picture. They never look closely at the model's face to see the color of his flesh tone. If the skin looks a little odd through your viewfinder, it will record that way on the film.

There are two easy ways to compensate for discoloration of the skin. The easiest way is to have the model move to a different position. If he is completely shaded, have him move to a point where the sun is filtering through a bit.

Sunlight and Fill Flash

The alternative is to use a method known as fill flash. A flash attachment is used to provide shadow-filling light which is of daylight color temperature. It will overpower the light reflecting from the grass and trees, and give the model a natural complexion color.

Cameras with leaf-type shutters allow for flash synchronization at any speed. Twin-lens reflexes, most Hasselblad cameras, special lenses for Bronica and Mamiya roll-film SLR cameras, and other equipment have this type of shutter. Most other cameras have just one speed at which flash can best be synchronized, and this is the setting you must use.

The first step when making a fill-flash picture in daylight is to take your normal light meter reading. Find out what f-stop you should use for the camera when the shutter is set on whatever speed your flash synchronization requires. This is usually somewhere between 1/60 and 1/125 second. When you take your light reading, find the f-stop that will enable you to use a shutter speed equal to the flash synchronization speed. For example, if your flash synchronization is set for 1/60 second and the light meter tells you that the normal exposure, without flash, is 1/60 at f/8, you're all right. If the light is so bright and the film of such speed that the normal reading is 1/250 at f/16, you cannot easily use the fill flash.

When shooting outdoors, a photographer cannot control the position of the sun. Photographers who do not have lighting systems often find it best to restrict their outdoor shooting sessions to overcast days (1) so that the sunlight lights the model's entire face rather than creating bright spots and shadows. An electronic flash can be used to supplement sunlight (2).

Figure your flash-to-subject distance normally once you are certain that you can use the shutter speed that matches your normal exposure without flash. If you are so close that the f-stop you will need is smaller than your minimum f-stop on the lens (f-22 is needed, for example, and f-16 is the minimum f-stop for your lens), you will have to move the flash farther back. A long flash cord will help in such a circumstance.

You can reduce the light output also by placing a single fold of handkerchief over the lens. Some photographers say they use one fold per f-stop for light reduction; others say the reduction of light is much greater when two or three folds are used rather than one. Actually, the light reduction varies with the construction of the flash and its power, the thickness of the handkerchief, and other variables. This is a technique with which you should experiment before you actually use it with the model. Take a full roll of film and vary exposures with each thickness of a clean white cloth or handkerchief. (Place the cloth in a plastic bag between uses so dust doesn't darken it enough to change its light-transmitting properties.)

Ideally, you should get the f-stop required for the fill flash as close as you can to the f-stop you would use for available-light photography. When the fill light matches the daylight, all you are doing is adding color-controlled light to the subject's face. You are eliminating the purple effects caused by reflections from leaves and grass without overpowering the daylight.

Artificial Available Light

After having taken many photographs of models illuminated by sunlight, you might decide to try working with artificial available light indoors. If so, you must know what kind of light—sunlight, tungsten, fluorescent—will be available,

and then select an appropriate film. If your subject is to be lighted by sunlight coming through a window, use daylight film. If the light is from tungsten (household) bulbs, use tungsten film. Experiment with different films if the light is a mixture of sunlight and tungsten. Fluorescent light presents some problems. There are some brands of film that work better than others in fluorescent light, but even these tend not to be able to completely eliminate the characteristic green cast.

The only way to effectively use color film with fluorescent lighting is to attach a filter to your lens. Fluorescent light correction filters sold commercially provide excellent, though not perfect, color correction. Professionals who regularly encounter fluorescent lights often buy a color temperature meter and a stack of colored gelatin filters. The special meter, which can cost several hundred dollars, shows what slight addition of some magenta, orange, and other colors of filtration must be used to make a custom filter perfectly compatible with the film-light combination. Then they mount the several gelatin filters in a special holder, attach it to the lens (you can even hold them in front of other types of cameras) and know that the color of the final image will be flawless. This is expensive and impractical. When you see fluorescent fixtures, either take black-and-white images or buy the inexpensive, commercially made general correction filter. Everything else is a waste of time and money (except for professionals handling interior photography and similar assignments requiring perfect color reproduction).

Lighting Techniques

Whichever kind of light you use, the secret to good model lighting technique is to watch your model, not your lights. If you have ever read a book on

lighting, you have seen diagrams indicating proper lighting techniques for each facial type. You have read about "butterfly lighting," "hatchet lighting," "Rembrandt lighting," and similar arrangements—each of which is supposed to serve a specific purpose. What most photography writers fail to say is that while these methods should be considered general guides—they are covered in detail later in this chapter—they must not be followed rigidly. The purpose of proper lighting is to make the model look his best. This might require one light or six, and you might use normal room lighting, quartz-halogen bulbs, electronic flash or almost anything else. All that matters is the final effect.

You can't change the position of the sun, so working with sunlight leaves much beyond your control. Electronic flash most often leaves you without a way to predict how the light will strike the model's face. Therefore, the best type of lighting to use when studying the effects of light on a model's body and face is tungsten light in the form of regular room lights or spotlights. Here are our suggestions of ways in which you can perfect your lighting technique using tungsten light. What you learn by doing this will prove valuable when you take other photographs using the sun or electronic flash.

Take a light in your hand or position it so that it is three or four feet from your model. Have the model close his eyes, then turn on the bulb and study the result of this direct lighting. Note how shadows exaggerate or diminish certain features—especially the eyes, nose, and mouth. Raise and lower the light, studying how the changing angles alter the face. Move the light a few inches to the left or right, then a few inches more. Once you have finished this study—and it should take only two or three minutes—place the light at whatever angle makes the model look most attractive. This is your main or "key" light. Every other light you use will be positioned in relation to the key light.

Photographers using straight flood lighting invariably use two lights, and many use three. The two-light minimum is suggested because the key light, no matter how carefully placed, will create a certain amount of shadowing which is not complimentary to the model. This shadowing is eliminated or reduced to a more attractive level by the fill light.

The fill light is never as strong as the key light. However, this does not mean that it should be a weaker bulb. The amount of light striking a subject is determined by the power of the bulb and the distance from the bulb to the subject. If the key light and fill light are exactly the same distance from your model, the fill light should be less bright. For example, a 500-watt key light might be used with a 250-watt fill light. Two 500-watt lights could be used for key and fill illumination by moving one light further back than the other. The key light might be five feet from the model, and the fill light

six or seven feet away.

Every time you use a controlled background such as a wall or seamless paper (discussed later), you can eliminate shadows, including those caused by front lighting, by overwhelming the shadow with more light. Position one, two or more lights outside the angle of view of the lens. Aim the lights toward the backdrop, shining enough light on the backdrop so that the shadow image created by the key light is overwhelmed by the secondary light.

A fill light positioned next to the camera and aimed directly at the model's face produces what is known as frontal or "pancake" lighting. Everything is flattened; the nose is seemingly pushed back into the face. Shadows are projected onto the background. You achieve the flash-on-camera effect so familiar in amateur snapshots. Shadowing on the face is eliminated, so attractive contouring with light cannot be achieved.

Move the light to the side so that an imaginary angle created by a line drawn from the light to the subject and back to the

camera forms an angle of 45 degrees. This is called (what else?) 45-degree lighting. The side of the face receiving the full force of the light will look flat. The other side of the face will be shadowed. The result is more effective than pancake lighting. There is still a shadow visible behind the model, but this can be handled by raising the light so that it is also angled slightly downward.

Another technique of direct lighting is known as Rembrandt lighting, named for the famous artist. The light remains at the same height at which it was first placed to achieve the most flattering position for 45-degree lighting. Then the light is moved so that it is from 130 to 160 degrees away from the camera. Most of the light is lost to the camera, since it falls on the side of the face farthest from the camera's position. Rembrandt lighting can illuminate a portion of the model's face—usually the forehead, nose, mouth, and chin. The eye catches some of the illumination, especially if the model is seen in profile. Profile work is the most effective with this type of lighting. The

Light from different angles can be used to "sculpture" a model's face. Pancake lighting (1) is often the least attractive.

Moving the light source to one side or the other at an angle of 45 degrees from the camera creates 45-degree

lighting (2). Rembrandt lighting (3) requires that the light source be moved 130 to 160 degrees from the camera.

Interesting but not always flattering is hatchet lighting (1). It can be dramatic, but it can also exaggerate the subject's facial features. Butterfly lighting (2) is named for the shape of the shadow that appears under the subject's nose. Backlighting (3) is not meant to show the face.

model usually positions his head for a three-quarter or full-profile view.

One of the more interesting but often least flattering light styles is hatchet lighting. The model faces the camera and the light is positioned to form a 90-degree angle (again by running an imaginary line from light to model to camera). Hatchet lighting is also known as side lighting or texture lighting. Because there is much contrast between the two sides of the subject's face, the lighting can offer a visually fascinating study in both skin tones and shading. Side or hatchet lighting allows for a sharp, potentially dramatic contrast of light and dark. It has been used with models for advertising work. It quickly attracts the viewer's attention. However, it also tends to exaggerate features in an uncomplimentary manner.

Do you find a butterfly-shaped shadow under the nose an appealing sight? If you do, you will want to use butterfly or glamour lighting. The light is placed in front of a model, though enough to the side to avoid the horrors of front-lighting techniques. The light is raised slightly so that the nose causes a shadow to appear just above the upper lip. This shadow is shaped something like the silhouette of a butterfly. This lighting approach can also be used with the model turned away from the camera, including the profile. Do not position the head so low or the light so angled as to cause a thick shadow to cover both lips and darken the eyes.

The trouble with butterfly lighting is that it does not fit every face. Many women and men look foolish with the butterfly on their lips. Unfortunately, because butterfly lighting is also called glamour lighting, many glamour specialists choose to use it with every model they photograph. They give no thought to the person's face, which may be quite different from the type that would be most effectively handled with this lighting. If the model does not look glamorous when they are finished, they say that the model is either unattractive or lacks what it takes to be a professional model. In reality, the photographer lacks the sense to study the model, lighting him for what would make the person most attractive.

Rim lighting is the last of the distinct lighting styles that record the entire face. The light source is positioned farther behind the head of the subject than it would be for Rembrandt lighting so only a thin line of light appears on the model's head. Usually, this technique is used exclusively with black-and-white film and the exposure is a compromise. The rim of light becomes almost completely washed out and the shadow area is given enough exposure to reveal some flesh detail. The shadow area is allowed to go almost black when printed.

Backlighting is not meant to show the face. This approach separates the model from the background. The light is kept close enough to the model to shine through her hair, creating a halo effect. However, the exposure is set for the model's face and a second light is used to bring out facial details. The light shining through the model's hair should be of greater intensity than the front light. This insures that the halo effect will be retained. If the key light is equal to or stronger than the backlight, the lighting will seem normal.

Color Portfolio

Success in shooting color depends somewhat on the photographer's skill in using the equipment, and perhaps more so on the photographer's "eye"—the ability to see through the viewfinder each and every detail that will be recorded on film.

LIGHTING CANDIDS

Photographers who take candid shots are not always able to get close enough to their subjects to take a meter reading of the light falling on the subject. So when preparing for this picture, the photographer stepped into the sun to read the amount of light that hit his own hand, adjusted his camera for that light level, then stepped back into the shade to snap the shutter.

STOPPING ACTION

During many types of movement,
there is a point at which the action
stops for a fraction of a second.
Here the model's dog has reached
the midpoint of his jump: He has
finished moving upward and hasn't
yet started to move downward. The
photographer timed his pressing of
the shutter button to coincide
perfectly with this peak action.

PREFOCUSING FOR MOVEMENT

When planning a candid photograph
of a subject moving rapidly toward
the camera, the photographer
focused his camera lens on a spot a
few steps ahead of the runner. He
pressed the shutter button as the
subject reached that spot.

FRAMING THE MODEL

By searching for and using outdoor scenery that effectively frames the model, the photographer created images (1, 2, 3) much stronger than those that would have resulted had the model been isolated in a wide-open area. During each of the sessions, the photographer encouraged the model to relate to her surroundings, thus helping her to forget about the camera and relax.

OUTDOOR PROPS

The color and sense of perspective added to this picture (left) by the popcorn wagon heightens interest. Although the wagon dominates the photo, it also draws the viewer's attention to the model.

POSING OF HANDS

In portrait work, a model's hands can be positioned in various ways to convey different moods. The model's facial expression may not change significantly from one pose to the next (1, 2, 3), but the use of the hands gives each picture a unique look.

1

2

3

POSING

The mark of an experienced model (and an experienced model photographer, who can provide adequate direction) is the ability to assume attractive, natural-looking poses. Whether outdoors (1) or indoors in a studio setting (2), the position of the model's arms and torso greatly affect the overall look of the photo.

1

1

POSING

If the model asks, "What should I do with my hands?" the photographer might suggest the use of a simple prop, such as a purse (1) or jewelry.

POSING

A skilled model and a skilled photographer will work together --the model quickly assuming a succession of poses (2, 3, 4, 5) and the photographer shooting when the most attractive ones are found. During the session, many photographers continually speak words of encouragement to the model along with instructions. The session becomes almost a dance instead of drudgery.

2

3

4

5

2

3

POSING

As the model changes positions, perhaps moving gradually from a sitting to a half-reclining pose (1, 2, 3), the photographer must try to remain aware of all factors--the hair, clothing, expression, and relaxed look of the arms and legs. The overall pose might be fine, but a distracting detail, such as a lock of hair out of place, can ruin the shot.

USING SUNLIGHT

When shooting outdoors, the photographer can't change the position of the sun in the sky, but he can change the model's position to assure the best pose. If dark shadows obliterate attractive details of the model's face, she can be asked to turn her body slightly so the sunlight strikes her face at a different angle. Of course, such shadows may add drama to a photo and thus be desirable.

LIGHTING

Outdoors in lush surroundings, a model's skin can take on a purplish color--the result of sunlight being reflected off the greenery (1). To prevent this, the photographer must look closely at the image in the camera's viewfinder, remembering that the coloration seen there will most likely record on the film.

PORTRAITS

When shooting through foliage to soften a portrait, the photographer must remain observant. Does a leaf (2) or branch cut into the image of the model? Does sunlight through the foliage create unwanted shadows and bright spots (3) on her face? To avoid the problems of too-bright sun and too-dark shadows, many photographers who shoot portraits outdoors choose to do so on overcast days (4).

1

2

3

4

PORTRAITS

For optimal control over lighting and coloration, many photographers who take portraits work indoors in a studio setting. Under such a controlled condition, the photographer and model can concentrate fully on the pose and facial expression.

Trying Some Experiments

After having spent a good deal of time mastering the basics of model photography, you might want to experiment with soft-focus portraiture, introduce props into your sessions, or try your hand at photographing fashion shows. Each will give you an opportunity to expand your skills—and, as we'll see in the next chapter, to increase the size of your audience and therefore improve your chances of turning your hobby into a money-making venture.

Soft-Focus Portraits

There was a time when all portraits were "soft," that is, slightly out of focus, either completely or just around the edges. This was caused by the poor quality of most early optical glass. As lenses improved, sharpness increased. The quality of reproduction became flawless. However, people are not flawless. The ability of today's camera lenses to accurately record every minute detail of a person's face often means that uncomplimentary blemishes and wrinkles are recorded sharply along with such details as pleasant character lines and long eyelashes. Soft-focus techniques are therefore used to erase some of the unwanted details while preserving the wanted ones. The overall look of a soft-focus portrait is less harsh than that of one taken without special softening. By mastering the art of soft-

focus, you'll be able to seemingly subtract years from your model's age or in other ways make the resulting image very

appealing to the model. An almost imperceptible amount of softening can impress a model enough to encourage him or her

A variety of soft-focus techniques can be used to soften the entire image or just the edges, leaving the center sharp.

to work with you again. A greater degree of softening can create a special mood—dreaminess, tranquility, romance.

Special lenses are available to the portrait photographer interested in taking soft portraits. Such lenses may be adjustable from normal sharpness if desired to so soft as to seem almost out of focus at the other extreme. But soft-focus lenses are relatively expensive and so specialized that you may want to find an alternative to them.

A cheap approach is the use of a clear optical glass filter (A UV or daylight-type filter can be purchased if you cannot find one made of clear optical glass). Carefully smear a thin layer of petroleum jelly over the outer surface of the filter (not the side of the filter that will come closest to the camera lens), leaving a clear spot in the center. The filter can be washed and then dried with lens cleaning tissues without serious damage. If the filter should be accidentally scratched or broken, it can be inexpensively replaced. A camera lens cannot be washed without harm, and any attempts at removing petroleum jelly could damage the surface coating. The thicker the layer of petroleum jelly on the filter, the greater the diffusion of light and the softer the image.

An alternative to the use of a filter with petroleum jelly is to take a nylon stocking and pull it over the lens. Pull it taut and fasten it with a rubber band. This will force the holes far enough apart to allow you to focus through it. The stocking will break up the image and create an overall softness.

Another approach is to use a piece of waxed paper held over the lens with a rubber band. Cut a hole in the center of the paper before mounting it on the lens. Focusing is done through the hole. Two or three layers of clear plastic food wrap, preferably crinkled in your hand before mounting, can do the same job.

No matter what type of on-

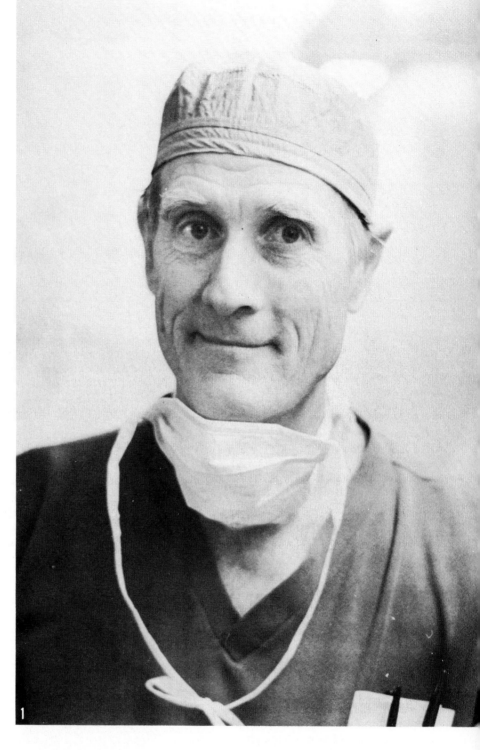

camera diffuser you use, the technique for using it is the same. Move close to the model to limit how much of his face is sharp; move back to make the entire face sharp. Everything in the image outside the view of the center hole will be softened. If lights are visible in the picture,

their glow will be softened.

Experiment also with small pieces of window screen, pieces of patterned acrylic sheets, and the translucent plastic wrap that is used in the packaging material for stereo equipment. (Also try shooting through a window on which you have sprayed

2

Environmental portraits can be taken with the model at work (1) or at home (2), dressed either in work clothes or casually as when relaxing. The available light might be sufficient for photography. If not, an electronic flash can be used to provide adequate light.

the model's home to convey some interesting aspect of his or her personality. Photograph your subject in an area of his home that is most appropriate. This might be in a study, at a desk, in a kitchen, or even at work in the garden. The clothing selected might range from very casual to semiformal. A teenager might be photographed while sprawled on the floor of his bedroom, surrounded by posters and recordings. An educator or professional person might be pictured in shirt and tie when relaxing, the suit-coat or sports jacket having been removed. That same person might normally switch into jeans and an old T-shirt the moment he comes home from work. If so, that is the way to photograph him. You do not have to own a complex lighting system to handle the casual home portrait, though it would help. Instead, you can move room lights to strategic places.

Outdoor environmental photographs are easier than indoor ones. Many people have unusual gardens or other outside locations where they will want to be photographed. Pick a time of day when the light is at such an angle that you can work without flash or other supplementary illumination. Usually, this means before 10 A.M. and after 2 P.M.

Another kind of "prop," so to speak, is a second person. Two people who can interact with each other, such as a couple on a date, probably will lose awareness of you and your camera and enable you to ob-

some hairspray, water, or light oil.)

A softened image can be created by taking your model outdoors and framing him with heavy foliage. He might stand in front of a tree, its leaves and branches framing his body. The leaves and twigs very close to the camera will be blurred, but the model's head will be in sharp focus.

Environmental Portraits and Props

For this type of model photography, you can use props from

tain some very interesting candid photographs.

Another way to take unusual pictures of models is to include a pet. Bring along a favorite toy, dog biscuits or other items to which a pet dog will react when you take the model and pet to the park or other scenic area. Photograph them while they play. (You will have to work quickly, because animals have relatively brief attention spans.) The spontaneous interaction leads to delightful reactions. Be ready for the unexpected, such as a dog rolling in the mud and then shaking the dirt onto the model. Also, be certain to position yourself so that the pet and model will always be in even lighting, preferably direct sun, as they romp near your camera. Dogs are the easiest to work with, but you can also use a horse or cat.

Fashion Shows

Fashion shows organized by famous designers are few in number, usually open only to members of the press and professional photographers, and perhaps a bit too ambitious a project for the amateur. Yet there are some fashion shows being organized in your community right now, no doubt, to which you can be invited.

For shows put on by small boutiques and department stores in small towns, the clothing is taken from the rack, the models are local people, and the event is held to bring the public into the store. The shows might be held in restaurants, shopping malls, local high school auditoriums or a room in the store. The photography is meant to be a record of the event, so amateur photographers often are given a chance to handle such an assignment. No matter what type of camera you have, you can take acceptable full-figure photos.

Much fashion modeling is called runway modeling, for the raised platform that extends in-to the audience. The model walks down this runway, often moving to the rhythm of music, stops at one end, turns and moves back. He or she might also pause part way down to show different accessories. There are moments when the movement stops. Such a situation works in your favor because it allows you to take a picture at the point when the model is still, and thus use any camera you might have. Stopping a model in motion often requires sophisticated flash equipment.

Shopping center and restaurant fashion shows usually do not use runway models, though they do use runway techniques. The model will walk to a predetermined spot, pause, pose, turn, and return to the changing area. In a restaurant, she will stop at every two or three tables, posing in the garment and talking a bit about the clothing and the store that sells it. Again you will have moments of peak action when the model is virtually still, so any camera can be used.

The first step toward photographing a fashion show is to learn when peak action will occur. You might want to ask the model prior to the show where she will pause. Position yourself so that you can take a full-frame photograph of the model at the point of peak action.

If you are using a flashcube-type camera, keep in mind that the flashcube will be almost completely ineffective when you are more than 10 feet from the model, and being closer than seven feet can be a problem because the cube may give off too much light.

Using any other camera, you can usually position yourself at any distance that allows you to record the full-figure model most effectively. You adjust the lens opening and focus accordingly. By using fast film (such as an ASA 400 color or black-and-white), even the simplest flash will allow you to obtain well-lighted photographs from 15 feet away. Powerful units can enable you to stand back more than twice this distance.

Flash photography for fashion shows is usually direct. Direct flash is all that is needed, despite the fact that the resulting photos will look flat and include shadows. The model is most likely to be in the open with enough space behind her to eliminate the shadow problem. If the model is near a curtain or wall, the shadow may be evident, but since you are working on a "grab-shot" basis, no one will object.

Some fashion shows are done in areas where floodlights are used, so you might be able to work with available light. This requires an adjustable-exposure camera.

The fashion model is always secondary to the clothing. You want to capture the clothing at its best, even if the model does not record perfectly. Clothing is most effectively recorded when you are at the same height as the model. If the model is on an elevated runway, try to stand on a similarly elevated object yourself, such as a sturdy chair. Try to avoid having to stand in the wings, recording the model as she moves off the stage. It is better to work from the audience because the model is at peak concentration when facing the onlookers. The model going off stage may stop smiling and relax in a way that causes the clothing to begin hanging in an unflattering manner.

In a restaurant, sit at one of the tables and then stand each time the model approaches. This keeps you in a position to catch all the action, yet avoid blocking anyone's view for more than a moment.

You will need permission to photograph a fashion show. To obtain it, contact the manager of the store or restaurant, or the sponsor of the show (which might be a modeling school or be the manufacturer of the clothing). Do not simply show up without an invitation.

Selling Your Photographs

The more you take pictures of people, the more you will probably find yourself looking through magazines and thinking that some of your work is as good as or better than what the professional photographers are doing. You probably have a print or slide that truly grabs everyone who views it. You've been wondering what you'd have to do to sell some of your pictures.

You are likely to have some salable photographs, and you might be able to sell enough of them to almost make your hobby pay for itself. You have the talent; now all you need is a sense of marketing.

There are three general markets for your photographs: organizations and businesses that hold fashion shows; the people who pose for you; and publications.

Selling to Businesses

One potential buyer of fashion photographs is the head of a store's fashion department. This person will have a budget for promotion that includes payment for photographs of the fashion show. Another possible buyer is the person in charge of advertising and/or public relations for the store or the designer involved. Sometimes the pictures are needed for advertising; other times they are records for cooperative advertising funds.

Many manufacturers are willing to work on a cooperative basis with department store

A photograph resulting from a visit to an organization's outing could be sold to the group as well as to the model.

advertising promotions. For example, a maker of casual fashions might be trying to promote its line of jeans. The advertising manager of the company notifies a large department store that if the store will spend $1,000 promoting the jeans, the company will provide matching funds. To obtain the matching funds, the department store will have to prove that it promoted the product; therefore, it might need to have photos taken of the fashion show it staged in which the jeans were featured. Some photographs can be sold to restaurants that stage fashion shows.

You should also talk with the restaurant' manager to see if there is an interest in having you photograph the "Employee of the Month." Once a month the employee to be honored is photographed in the restaurant, at your home studio or outdoors. The photo is displayed where the public can see it and might include your name in addition to that of the subject.

Another market is one that you create yourself. You can offer to print your people and model photographs for businesses to use for promotion. For example, a pretty waitress, perhaps holding a menu, can be printed on a calendar back for the coming year. Or the print might be placed on postcards or greeting cards. Sensitized materials for make-it-yourself calendars, postcards, and the like are available from many camera stores, either directly or by special order. If your store can't get them for you, one source is the mail order firm Porter's Camera Store, Box 628, Cedar Falls, IA 50613. Many custom labs offer such services. You can also use companies such as McGrew Color Graphics, P.O. Box 19716, Kansas City, MO 64141. Neither of these businesses is recommended over others. They are among several that offer this type of work.

Calendars of attractive models can be sold as items to be given away by companies. Local modeling schools and agencies might also be interested. The potential is limited only by your imagination in locating businesses and adapting your work to their special interests.

Selling to Models

You might find that the store-sponsored fashion show provides an opportunity to sell two copies of each photo—one to the business and one to the model. Often the models who take part in such a show will pay

Perhaps a shot that looks as though it belongs on a calendar (1) can become a calendar. Businessess and modeling schools are two of the potential buyers. A restaurant sponsoring a fashion show or an organization sponsoring a wine-tasting might be interested in a photograph that could be used to advertise the event (2). An attractive model photographed in attractive outdoor surroundings (3) could be of interest to the model, a travel agency, a travel magazine.

to have a record of themselves as they appeared in it, either as a souvenir or to use as part of a portfolio. When a group of high school students working for a department store puts on a fashion show, the mothers of the students are often delighted to buy photographic records of the event.

Chances are good that some of the students who model these fashions aspire to continue modeling either as a hobby or a profession. These students will need portfolios which will show their prospective clients what they have to offer. Modeling portfolio work sold through high schools and colleges will usually have to be developed through advertising in school newspapers. If you are a student, word of mouth also helps with sales. You might even be allowed to display some of your prints in the student union or other central location, along with a business card. If you work through a modeling school, its director might help to promote you, since someone both competent and able to take extra time with beginners is always welcome.

To display your skills as a photographer, you also will need a portfolio. Prepare one containing your photographs, preferably 8 x 10 in size, both black-and-white and color. Select photographs that show the full range of your abilities. Keep in mind that people tend to buy what they see. If you have a combination of outdoor portraits and home studio pictures, potential customers will consider asking you to do both for them. If you have only outdoor portraits, the people you encounter will never think about asking you for more formal work taken indoors.

One successful way to sell your services is as a neighborhood, school, business or even apartment-complex photographer. Many camera buffs living in large apartment complexes offer their services through small notices posted on bulletin boards in the laundry room or other center of activity. Home dwellers go door-to-door in their neighborhoods during early evenings and on weekends. Some people go so far as to buy advertisements in area newspapers; such an approach can be expensive if you want to work on only a casual basis.

Selling to Publications

Magazines that buy photographs comprise a number of categories. One of them is the category of trade journals which cater to a particular business or industry as well as to particular occupations. In the field of photography, for example, you might find *Studio Photography Magazine, Functional Photography Magazine, The Professional Photographer,* and several others. These are sold by subscription only, unlike hobby magazines which appear on the newsstands. *Popular Photography, Modern Photography, Petersen's Photographic Magazine* and *American Photographer* are among the hobby publications available to camera buffs.

Hobby magazines; publications for women such as *Working Woman, Ms.,* and others; and periodicals aimed at brides, skiers, and runners are known as special-interest publications. They have a narrow audience, confining themselves to a specialized field or set of circumstances.

The third major category of magazines are general-interest publications. These include such familiar periodicals as *Reader's Digest, Saturday Evening Post,* and *People.* The audience is assumed to include young and old men and women of all walks of life. They are meant to have the broadest possible appeal of all publications. They are also fewest in number. The special-interest field, with all its many divisions, is the largest.

You might think that the best place to send your pictures of people would be to the photography magazines; however, this probably is not correct. If you study these magazines, you will see that they need unusual photographs—pictures having a special theme or something else that makes them unique. A truly unusual image of a person taken with a simple fixed-focus camera on Kodachrome film will be readily accepted. (Other films can be used, but Kodachrome is the most easily reproducible color film in terms of color quality and grain structure for use in such cameras.)

If you want to try your luck with photography magazines, you should consider one or two approaches. If the magazine has a section reserved for readers' contributions, a single photograph fitting the magazine's needs might bring you $25 to $35. Those needs are explained in the specific section. Each picture must either stand on its own regardless of others run in the same issue or relate to a specific theme. *American Photographer* for example, sets a new theme each month; contributors have several weeks in which to submit something appropriate. Other magazines operate on the theory that if the picture is eye-catching and different, it is worth using regardless of how it relates to other images on the same page. Study the magazine before sending anything.

Another seemingly obvious market is the field of women's magazines. *Vogue, Seventeen, Glamour, Essence, McCall's,* and numerous other publications are filled with photographs

A model can be used to display the work of a local craftsman, and the photo might find a market in a local magazine.

of attractive women. However, if you look closely at the accompanying text, you will find that each photograph features a particular person in a specially coordinated outfit, hair-do, and makeup. All images are tied directly to either a particular article or an advertising promotion. Your subjects will lack such tie-ins.

So who, then, will be interested? Any magazine that uses pictures of attractive women or images of scenes in which people appear, that's who. Romance and confessions magazines, for example, regularly buy photos which show an attractive woman or a man and woman together for their covers and sometimes for inside use. Magazines aimed at the over-55 market often use scenic pictures; people pictures are fine. Religious magazines often buy pictures of people for their covers and inside use. An attractive picture will sell even if it doesn't relate to a specific article or story.

Before sending photographs anywhere, you should know what kinds of photos are being purchased by whom. A large magazine stand and the periodical room of your public library are good places to start your study. Next check the annually updated *Writer's Market* and *Photographer's Market*, both published by Writer's Digest Books. These are filled with thousands of markets and include descriptions of each publication's editorial needs. Another market guide, not annually updated though revised periodically, is *Where & How to Sell Your Photographs* by the late Arvel Ahlers, published by Amphoto. The book contains a large section on free-lance photography sales which can be extremely beneficial.

When mailing samples of your work, several precautions must be taken. First, be certain your name and address are on the backs of the photographs. You should buy a rubber stamp with

this information, and a pad of black ink. Place each print face down on a smooth, hard surface. Ink the stamp and *lightly* apply it to the back. No more force should be used than is necessary to transfer the information. If possible, the stamping should be done on the reverse of a black section of the photo so the ink will not show through from the front. Do not stamp one print on top of the previous one. Stamp each one separately, then move it from the surface before stamping the next. Do not stack the pictures until the ink has dried.

Slides should also have your name and address on them. Again a stamp can be used, though this can be risky: You might slip and accidentally apply ink to the transparency itself. It is better to tape an appropriately sized label on the mount or print the information with a pen.

Slides are irreplaceable originals and there is a risk that they will be lost or damaged in the mail. You can have duplicates made, though these are often of poor quality unless you spend several dollars on each one. You can also have an internegative made so that prints and/or slides can be made from the internegative. This is also somewhat costly ($4 to $7) if the quality is high. Perhaps the best way to protect your slide is also the most expensive. This is through the use of a color separation negative. These are produced so that you have three black-and-white images, each photographed through a different color filter. When the three negatives are printed through similar filtration, the color image is restored. This procedure assures utmost permanence.

Unless a slide is unusually impressive, the cost of protecting it through quality color separations or even an internegative is probably higher than the potential revenue from its repeated sale. You are better off protect-

ing the transparencies by mailing them properly. This means using plastic sheets with appropriately sized pockets for holding individual slides. These sheets are punched for mounting in notebooks, making for easy storage. Each sheet holds 20 of the 2 x 2-inch slide mounts or from four to six 2¼ x 2¼-inch slides. Always buy the stiff, heavy-duty slide holders—the lightweight kinds tear too easily. Most camera stores handle such slide pages. Many hobby stores and shops that sell coins also carry them because they can be used for coin holders, which are of similar size; and the coin stores often sell them for prices slightly lower than those charged by camera stores.

Place only the specific slides you want to send in the plastic page without worrying about filling the entire holder. It is better to send two or three slides that are perfect for the market in a holder capable of holding 20 slides than to fill the holder with mostly inappropriate material and risk drawing the editor's attention away from the high-quality work.

The prints and/or slides should be placed in what are known as photo mailers. These are nothing more than large, heavy-duty envelopes containing two pieces of corrugated cardboard between which you place your material. You can make such a mailer by buying an appropriately sized envelope and cutting two pieces of corrugated cardboard to size. (Always use corrugated cardboard: Nothing of comparable weight affords better protection.)

Magazine production costs have risen drastically in recent years. Publishers and editors receive many submissions, the majority of which are inappropriate and have to be returned. If they were to pay for the return themselves, their costs could be prohibitive. The editors realize how expensive and valuable your work is to you, but they have had to adopt a hard-nosed attitude: Unless you make proper arrangements for getting it back, the work probably will not be returned. The publications want an appropriately sized return envelope which you have self-addressed and stamped with adequate postage for the return of the prints. This usually is an envelope of the same size as the mailing envelope, but doubled over. You slip the folded envelope inside the mailer so that it is with the prints and/or slides. If this is done, most publications will make every effort to return your work.

There is no need to insure your photographs, though you should always mail them First Class to be certain they travel the fastest way. If you do insure the work with the United States Postal Service and should the material be lost, you will probably not collect. This is not because the Postal Service distrusts photographers; rather, there is no way to set a value on what you have done beyond the cost of materials. If a photograph had sold for $100 each time to several magazines over the years, you could legitimately claim a market value of $100 for each resale you could realistically have made in the future. But if your photographs have never been sold before and may not prove appropriate for the magazine to which you have sent them, you cannot say they have a market value. Fortunately, the loss of First Class packages in the mail is negligible; most photographers go for years without ever experiencing any problems and many never have difficulties.

One caution: Be certain to mark both sides of your package "First Class" boldly and in *red ink*. Postal workers admit that large packages such as those used to mail photographs frequently are assumed to be Third Class, since most Third Class mail is of this size. Third Class mail is not handled as efficiently as is First Class.

Address an accompanying letter "To the Editor" and use a "Dear Editor" greeting which is non-sexist and safer than addressing an editor by name. The turnover in editorial personnel is so great among magazines that a name listed in a market guide or even in the staff box of a current magazine may no longer represent an employee of that publication.

Your letter should state that you are a professional photographer and you are submitting the enclosed "on speculation" at your "usual rates." Say you are professional, even if you had never considered selling a picture before and believe that you might not try to sell anything again. The reason for this is that some magazines pay different rates to amateurs than they do to professionals for comparable photos. Editors have been known to send letters saying something to the effect of this: "Normally we pay nothing [or $5, $10, or whatever] for free-lance submissions, but since you mentioned that you are a professional, we can offer you $50 for your picture." The amounts vary, of course, and this example is strictly hypothetical; but the situation is one of which you should be aware.

Free-lance submissions are considered and returned or purchased according to whatever schedule is convenient for the editor. Some publications respond within a day or two of receiving the material; others take six to eight weeks to reply. Assuming everything was mailed First Class for sending and return and that you included adequate postage, you should hear one way or another no more than two months after mailing. If more time passes, a polite query asking about the material and its current status should be sent. Be certain to include both your telephone number and a self-addressed, stamped reply envelope. This should be a regular-size envelope; not one large enough to hold the photographs.

Setting a Price

Magazines have set rates they pay for submitted photographs, but when you sell pictures to individuals such as your models, you'll have to set your own price. This can be a problem because most photographers do not know their true cost.

Cost is figured two ways, only one of which will be discussed in this book. If you were a professional, you would have to determine overhead as it relates to your studio. Such information is covered in detail in books such as Ted Schwarz's *How to Start a Professional Photography Business,* published by Contemporary Books, and sections of the Kodak *Encyclopedia of Practical Photography.* If you are advanced enough to be interested in this complex aspect of pricing, books such as the two mentioned would be worth studying. However, for the average person just trying to make a little money with his camera, figuring expenses is relatively simple.

The easiest way to figure your real costs for taking pictures is to list *every* expense that is directly related to the photo session with your subject. There is the cost of film and processing, including all mailing expenses if the film is sent out of town. There is the cost of special lighting equipment, if any; seamless paper; props, etc. For an item such as seamless paper, you should figure a percentage of its life. If the paper will last through sessions with 15 models, then your cost per model is 1/15 the price of a new roll. Other items have to be guessed, such as wear and tear on cameras.

Be certain to consider all angles. If film has to be purchased, gasoline is priced so high that you should include the cost of driving. Remember that the travel to and from the camera store would not have taken place had it not been for the pictures, so this is an expense.

Since you are not handling modeling work regularly or on a professional basis, you need not worry about determining overhead such as space rental, telephone, business cards, utilities, and the like.

Print costs must be considered as well. There is the cost of making the print and the cost of mailing if you use an out-of-town laboratory. Remember to include the cost of an envelope to hold the negatives when they are mailed to the lab. Such costs are so small that they are easy to forget; but they add up.

A professional studio generally marks up prices from three and a half to five and a half times in order to meet expenses and make a profit. Surprisingly, you would be wise to seriously consider the higher markup. The reason is that a professional will add full overhead—a percentage of rent, utilities, equipment, maintenance costs, and all the other factors that go into running a full-time business—to the original cost. The more you charge, without overpricing your work compared with studios in your area, the better and more realistic your profit.

Fashion shows are a professional venture even when you have a fixed-focus camera. Set a reasonable price for your work. Usually this is three and a half to five and a half times the cost of doing the work, plus an extra hourly fee for your time if you are on assignment. Since you might be just a beginner, you might be told, "Sure you can take pictures, and if we like what you show us when you're done, we might buy a few." This is too speculative for serious professionals, but may be just what you want when learning model photography.

MODEL RELEASES

There are two rules to follow when taking photographs of models and getting releases from them: One, shoot first and ask questions later; and two, it's better to be safe than sorry. Don't avoid taking a photograph of someone merely because you believe you'd have trouble obtaining a release, since releases are seldom necessary. But try to get releases whenever you can, because buyers of photos do sometimes ask for them.

Most magazines want to know if you have some sort of model release available. This can be a simple statement giving up all rights in exchange for a fee or a complex contract. Form releases are available through most camera stores. The simplest are printed on 3 × 5 cards and sold in a small pack. They are good to use at all times, even when you don't think you will ever try to sell anything.

A model release *must* be available when a photograph will be used for advertising or other promotional purposes; when the image will be distorted either visually or through a caption; when the image could be embarrassing, incriminating or otherwise cause serious problems for the subject (except for news pictures); and any situation in which the viewer would be misled about the subject.

Usually your sales will be to publications that will run your picture as simply an attractive image, so no release will be needed, though some editors prefer to have one anyway. If your photo of Sonia Sweetheart, your next-door neighbor, will run in a magazine with a caption that contains only her name and your name, Sam Snapshot, you won't need a release. But if the photo runs with the caption "Sonia Sweetheart says, 'Sam Snapshot is the greatest photographer in the whole world'," you will need a release. Likewise, a picture of an old man can be sold as a picture of an old man if his beard and craggy face more than confirm his age. But if you know him to be a wino and expect the picture to be run with a caption such as "Years of alcoholism show on the face of this old tramp," you will certainly need a release. Such a comment is derogatory; the man or his family could sue you.

One way to view the situation is that a model release is always best to have even though it is not always necessary. When you send a photograph to a publication, caption it accurately and in such a way that no one will feel libeled, maligned or otherwise troubled by it.

Stay with magazines that also are respected by others—do not send your picture of Sonia Sweetheart to any magazine whose reputation could damage hers.

Many photographers think a model must be paid when signing a release in order to make a legal contract. You may have heard that you must pay at least a dollar for the agreement to be binding, for example. The truth is that no money need change hands unless the release specifically states that such a condition is essential. However, many photographers prefer to pay at least a dollar for what they see as self-protection. Their feeling is that if someone signs a release and later claims he or she didn't understand what was being signed, a problem could arise; but when money changes hands, there is no way the person can realistically say that a business deal was not understood. The exchange of just a dollar makes for a safer relationship, though the money or lack of it has nothing to do with the legality of it all.

Never send an original model release with your photographs, even when it is requested. Instead, send a copy. You do not want the original to leave your possession.

Illustrated here is a sample release. The language of the agreement is similar to that of most releases. The signature of a witness is not needed unless the photograph will be used for advertising or other promotional purposes. If it will, anyone—a passerby on the street, for example—can witness the signing of the release by you and the model.

Some photographers who always try to get releases from their models carry such releases with them in their gadget bags wherever they go with their cameras.

Model Release

For valuable consideration, I hereby irrevocably consent to and authorize the use and reproduction by you, or anyone authorized by you, of any and all photographs which you have this day taken of me, negative or positive, proofs of which are hereto attached, for any purpose whatsoever, without further compensation to me. All negatives and positives, together with the prints shall constitute your property, solely and completely.

Model Name _____ Date _____
           Signature

Address _____ Phone _____

City _____ State _____ Zip Code _____

Signature of Parent or Guardian if Minor _____

Witnessed by _____
                   Signature

Buying New Equipment

A photographer's technique—his knowledge of posing, lighting, and the use of props—is at least as important to the taking of good people pictures as his equipment, if not more so. Nevertheless, as your technique improves you'll probably feel a continuing urge to add to and upgrade your system of camera(s) and accessories.

When the time comes for you to buy new equipment, refer to this chapter. These brief reviews do not cover every camera and accessory that the editors of CONSUMER GUIDE® magazine believe to be worthy of consideration; but, because of our direct experience in working with these and many other products for our photographic equipment test reports, we know the following to be good values.

CAMERAS

Single-Lens Reflex

Contax RTS. The Contax RTS is made to work interchangeably with the Yashica SLR line, sharing lens mount and many accessories. It is an excellent camera, offering the versatility found in most "systems" equipment. Interchangeable focusing screens are available, though the finder is permanent. The Contax RTS should be considered an extremely sophisticated second body when moving up in quality from a Yashica SLR camera which you have used for a few years. If you are buying your first SLR and want a more versatile and fairly priced line, the Olympus system would be better.

Minolta SRT-201. The Minolta system which includes the 201 rivals the Yashica and Contax systems in that it combines extremely inexpensive models with a body that is meant to be a true systems camera. The basic Minolta SRT-201 is one of the least costly SLRs available with a built-in light meter and lenses ranging from extreme wide-angle to a longer telephoto than you are ever likely to use. The 201 lacks an autowinder and interchangeable focusing screens. Minolta XK Motor Drive model has a built-in motor drive. Less expensive than the top-of-the-line XK are the Minolta XD-11, and the XG-6 and XG-7 cameras, all of which can use autowinders. This is a good system to own. However, the 201 lacks some of the valuable

features of the Olympus OM-1n, which sells for approximately the same price.

Nikon F2AS Photomic. The Nikon line is one of the oldest and most sophisticated camera systems ever made. It includes a vast array of lenses, interchangeable viewing screens, focusing screens, film backs, and other accessories far too numerous to mention. Equipment that functioned on the first Nikon F cameras still works on the most sophisticated models available today.

The Nikon Photomic is over-designed for most photographer's needs. It is a camera that can be used for scientific, industrial, and other purposes. Part of the relatively high cost is reflected in its tremendous versatility and adaptability. It has been on the market for well over 20 years. Older lenses and used camera bodies are readily available throughout the U.S.

Nikon FM. This is one of the least expensive of the newer Nikons. It has mechanical shut-

Contax RTS 35mm Single-lens-reflex camera.

Nikon FM 35mm SLR.

Olympus OM-2n 35mm single-lens reflex.

ter speeds. The metering system is extremely sensitive and accurate. The camera takes a motor drive (three and a half frames per second versus three frames per second for the Olympus power winder and five frames per second for the Olympus motor drive) which is adequate for modeling work and most sports. However, neither the focusing screen nor the finder housing is removable, as they are on the Nikon F2AS. Other features are similar to the most sophisticated Nikons.

Olympus OM-1n and **OM-2n.** These are updated versions of the camera that revolutionized photographic equipment design a few years ago. It was the first small systems camera, and its mirror was so well dampened that it was almost as quiet as the Leica M series rangefinder cameras.

The Olympus OM-1n accepts a wide range of high-quality optics, can be equipped with both a motor drive and a power winder, and offers interchangeable focusing screens. Such focusing screens are extremely important when certain specialized lenses are used. (They also can be useful should your vision change with the passing years.) The Olympus OM-1n has an extremely sensitive metering system which is independent of the shutter.

Should the meter battery go dead, the shutter will still operate at all speeds. It is mechanical rather than electronic—a design which will seem unimportant until you are in the middle of an assignment and the batteries die.

The OM-2n is similar to the OM-1n, except that the former has an electronic shutter. The electronic shutter is battery-dependent, but allows time exposures of up to two minutes in low-light situations. Therefore, a model who stands motionless can be photographed by a tripod-mounted Olympus OM-2n at night using only the built-in meter to measure the light accurately. You also have the option of manual override of the metered information, plus overexposure and underexposure options.

Because the new Olympus cameras have been changed slightly from their predecessors and carry the "n" designation, earlier models are available at low prices. One of the earlier models bought used will serve you the rest of your life if you give it proper care and maintenance. (Be aware that models of the early OM-1 that do not bear the designation "MD" will not be adaptable to the motor drive and power winder—a disadvantage if you eventually want to photograph fast-moving subjects.)

Yashica FR-II. This is a well-made, inexpensive, basic 35mm SLR. It has a relatively noisy shutter, a noninterchangeable viewing screen and finder, and an automatic shutter. When the battery goes dead, you must either have a spare handy in your gadget bag or lose all but one shutter speed.

CAMERAS

35mm Rangefinders

Canon G-III 17. The G-III 17 is a compact unit with big-camera potential. It is a precision instrument. The "17" in the Canonet's name stands for the maximum lens aperture of f/1.7. That aperture allows the camera to be used in low-light situations. The Canonet's rangefinder is quite large for cameras of this type. Focusing by means of the coincident images is easy and precise.

The camera's automatic exposure system uses a built-in CdS meter. Its sensor eye is located above the lens. The Canonet allows full manual control. You can use the meter for automatic exposure or make your own settings. A range of shutter speeds from 1/4 to 1/500 second and apertures from f/1.7 to f/16 give you just about all the versatility you'd need most of the time.

This Canon is one of the best examples of how the capabilities of a big camera can be condensed into a small camera. We believe the Canonet G-III 17 is an excellent value.

Olympus 35 RC. The 35 RC provides perhaps the best group of features available on any small rangefinder. As befits a company that has been so influencial in the development of small cameras, the Olympus 35 RC is an excellent example of camera miniaturization. The camera's body is beautifully finished. Every part of it shows painstaking attention to detail.

The camera's built-in CdS meter cell is located within the cylinder that contains the lens.

Four recommended cameras: Yashica FR-II 35mm SLR (1), Canonet G-III 35mm rangefinder (2), Olympus 35 RC rangefinder (3), Bronica ETRS medium-format camera (4).

This placement enables the meter to take into account and compensate for such accessories as filters that may be placed over the lens.

The rangefinder is very clear. It contains displays of shutter speeds and lens apertures, a low-light warning signal, a frameline for composition, and parallax correction marks. The RC uses the shutter-priority exposure control system. You set the shutter at any speed from 1/15 to 1/500 second, and the meter sets the aperture from f/2.8 to 4/22. The user has the option of full manual exposure control, a feature much to our liking.

This small Olympus is an outstanding camera in a crowded field.

CAMERAS
Medium Format

Bronica ETR S. When Bronica set out to design the ETR several years ago, the goal was to combine 35mm handling with 2¼-inch quality. Bronica was successful.

The genius behind the ETR S is obvious when the camera is dressed up with AE-2 finder, which converts the viewing system from waist-level to eye-level, and the speed grip—a right-handed, two-stroke film wind lever with flash hot shoe built in. The camera back, containing the film chamber, can be removed after insertion of a dark slide. In this way, two or more different sizes or types of film can be used alternately. The

Bronica ETR's 2¼ × 2¾-inch format allows for 15 exposures on a roll of 120 film; 30 exposures on a roll of 220.

Mamiya M645 1000S. This is another of the medium-format cameras that are rapidly rivaling the 35mm system as a popular format with both amateurs and professionals. The frame size is 60 × 45mm, making it a format which enlarges full frame to an 8 × 10-inch print.

The Mamiya M645 1000S is in the same price range as one of the higher-priced system 35mm SLRs such as the Nikon or Canon. It has behind-the-lens metering, interchangeable focusing hoods and viewfinders, a broad range of lenses, and even a motor drive.

The one disadvantage of the

Mamiya M645 1000S medium-format camera.

Soligor MK-10A automatic flash with bounce-flash head.

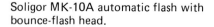

Mamiya over its nearest and slightly more expensive rival, the Bronica ETR, at this point is that the Mamiya M645 1000S has interchangeable film holders; the Bronica has completely interchangeable backs. A film back can be removed mid-roll and a new roll used, allowing you to switch from color slides to black-and-white to color negative film or whatever your preference, without ever losing a frame. The Mamiya interchangeable inserts allow a preloading of film for speedy change, but each roll must be completed or frames will be lost.

LIGHTING EQUIPMENT

Electronic Flash

Soligor MK-10A. This unit is a lot of flash for the money. A great deal of versatility is built into its compact body.

The body is split at about the one-quarter mark. The upper three-quarters contains the reflector; the lower portion contains the sensor eye in a large circular knob. Four colored dots around the knob indicate the various auto aperture settings available. You can unplug the sensor and replace it with an ac-

cessory cord for remote use. A large calculator wheel on the back of the top section has color-coded wedges for the auto modes. The dial is easily set by means of the knurled edge around its top, and clicks into position.

The unit's large foot can be swiveled in either direction to orient the flash horizontally. Then, by swiveling the reflector section, you can achieve three different bounce positions. A large black-and-white diagram on the exposed top portion of the bottom indicates the angle of the bounce.

Berkey-Colortran light stands. The Berkey-Colortran is super sturdy. It can be fully extended with a heavy quartz light and a large umbrella reflector without becoming top-heavy. You can bump it and mildly abuse it without fearing it will go crashing down on someone's head. It is quite expensive compared with other stands and probably is not something you'll want to purchase unless you wish to devote considerable time to your pursuit or try to go professional.

Smith-Victor lighting equipment. Smith-Victor is one of a number of companies that make medium-priced, good-quality lighting equipment. Most of what you will find in camera stores around the country is meant for flood bulbs and will cost a third or a fourth the price of a good Berkey-Colortran stand. It will also be less sturdy. A fully extended Smith-Victor lighting unit complete with reflector and bulbs but without an umbrella reflector is fairly sturdy.

Spiratone lighting equipment. Spiratone is a mail-order photographic equipment company that offers an excellent line of both floodlighting and quartz lighting equipment at low prices. The stands are reasonably sturdy, though not quite as good as those offered by Smith-Victor. A range of reflector umbrellas is also available.